20 EVENTS

Leaders

WHO CHANGED THE 20TH CENTURY

JODINE MAYBERRY

D1530096

RSVP

**RAINTREE
STECK-VAUGHN**

P U B L I S H E R S

The Steck-Vaughn Company

Austin, Texas

Consultant: Gary Gerstle, Department of History, The Catholic University of America

Developed for Steck-Vaughn Company by
Visual Education Corporation, Princeton, New Jersey

Project Director: Jewel Moulthrop
Assistant Editor: Emilie McCardell
Researcher: Carol Ciaston
Photo Research: Photosearch, Inc.
Production Supervisor: Maryellen Filipek
Proofreading Management: Amy Davis
Word Processing: Cynthia C. Feldner
Interior Design: Lee Grabarczyk
Cover Design: Maxson Crandall
Page Layout: Maxson Crandall, Lisa R. Evans

Raintree Steck-Vaughn Publishers staff

Editor: Shirley Shalit
Project Manager: Joyce Spicer

Library of Congress Cataloging-in-Publication Data

Mayberry, Jodine
    Leaders who changed the 20th century / Jodine Mayberry
        p.   cm. — (20 Events)
    Includes bibliographical references and index.
    Summary: Presents biographical sketches of twenty people who made significant contributions to the history of the twentieth century, including Jane Addams, Ho Chi Minh, Lech Walesa, and Nelson Mandela.
    ISBN 0-8114-4926-2
    1. Heads of state—Biography—Juvenile literature.
2. Statesmen—Biography—Juvenile literature.   3. Biography—20th century—Juvenile literature.   4. World politics—20th century—Juvenile literature.   [1. Biography—20th century.   2. Heads of state.   3. Statesmen.   4. World politics—20th century.]   I. Title.   II. Series.
D412.6.M37 1994   93–19032
920′.009′04—dc20   CIP
                                             AC

Cover: Martin Luther King, Jr., and Coretta Scott King (inset) led the Selma, Alabama, voting rights march in 1965. A crowd of 250,000 (background) gathered at the Washington Monument on August 28, 1963, when King gave his famous "I Have a Dream" speech.

Credits and Acknowledgments
Cover photos: UPI/Bettmann (background),
    © Bob Adelman/Magnum Photos (inset)
Illustrations: American Composition and Graphics
Maps: Parrot Graphics

4: George Eastman House (left), Sophia Smith Collection, Smith College (right); **5:** George Hirose/Henry Street Settlement; **6:** Library of Congress; **7:** Library of Congress (left), George Holton/Photo Researchers (right); **8:** Library of Congress; **9:** Reuters/Bettmann; **10:** The Bettmann Archive; **11:** Mark Boulton/Photo Researchers (left), George Ballis/Take Stock (right); **12:** UPI/Bettmann; **13:** Yivo Institute for Jewish Research (left), Cham/Sipa Press (right); **14:** Keystone Press; **15:** Imperial War Museum; **16:** AP/Wide World (left), UPI/Bettmann (right); **17:** U.S. Department of the Interior; **18:** UPI/Bettmann; **19:** U.S. Army/Wide World; **20:** Sovfoto/Eastfoto (left), Peter Hsu (right); **21:** Paolo Koch/Photo Researchers; **22:** Vietnam News Agency; **23:** UPI; **24:** Hamilton Wright/Photo Researchers (right); **25:** Sipa Press (left), The Bettmann Archive (right); **26:** UPI/Bettmann (left), Ann Purcell/Photo Researchers (right); **27:** Bud Lazarus; **28:** The Bettmann Archive; **29:** Reuters/Bettmann (left), Sovfoto/Eastfoto (right); **30:** UPI/Bettmann (left), UPI/Bettmann (right); **31:** Bob Black/*Chicago Sun Times*/Sipa Press; **33:** National Archives (left), Shlomo Arad/Sipa Press (right); **34:** UPI/Bettmann; **35:** Reuters/Bettmann (left), Reza/Sipa Press (right); **36:** Morvan/Sipa Press; **37:** Private Collection/W. W. Norton; **38:** UPI/Bettmann (left), Reuters/Bettmann (right); **40:** White House Photo (left), Reuters/Bettmann (right); **41:** Michael Rondou/*San Jose Mercury News*/Sipa Press; **42:** Reuters/Bettmann; **43:** Reuters/Bettmann

Contents

Jane Addams

As a social reformer, she worked in America's slums to improve the lives of the urban poor.

Following the British Model

In the late 1800s, the United States was a growing and prosperous nation. But only a few factory owners and industrial giants enjoyed this prosperity. For those who worked in the factories, conditions were quite different. Factory jobs attracted millions of people, mostly European immigrants, to America's cities. They lived in dark, airless tenements without clean water or proper sanitation. Men, women, and children worked long hours in factories and sweatshops for wages that barely supported them.

One of the people to recognize the problems of the urban poor was Jane Addams. The daughter of a wealthy Quaker banker in Illinois, Addams belonged to the first generation of college-educated women in America. Addams decided to study medicine. However, ill health forced her to leave medical school early. A few years later, while traveling in Europe with a friend, Ellen Gates Starr, Addams became interested in the new settlement movement. This movement was based on the idea that to help the poor, reformers should live among them. Addams and Starr visited the first settlement house, Toynbee Hall, in London. They decided to open a settlement house in the United States.

Her wealthy background and education enabled Jane Addams to dedicate her life to helping others.

Long hours and unsafe conditions for child factory workers were among the abuses that Addams sought to eliminate.

A Reformer's Career

Jane Addams and Ellen Gates Starr founded their settlement house in 1889 in Chicago's 19th Ward. The neighborhood was crowded with 5,000 Greek, Russian, Italian, and German immigrants. The women bought a crumbling old mansion that had once belonged to Charles Hull, a wealthy merchant. Hull House, as they called their establishment, became the most famous settlement house in the world.

By 1893, more than 2,000 people a day were coming to Hull House for help. Addams assembled a dedicated staff who ran a day nursery, a clinic, a playground, a gymnasium, and a boardinghouse for single working women. The center offered a variety of educational activities, including English, sewing, and cooking classes. Cultural activities included theater performances, art and music classes, and concerts.

Seeking New Laws Addams soon realized that the programs at Hull House did not solve the immigrants' most pressing social problems. She began to organize citizens and to lobby state and local governments for legal reforms.

In 1893, Jane Addams convinced the Illinois legislature to pass the nation's first law to inspect factories for safety. She also successfully lobbied for laws to abolish child labor, to limit the working day for women to eight hours, and to require school attendance for children. Through her efforts, Chicago established the first juvenile court in the United States in 1899.

Suffrage and Peace Jane Addams wrote several books about her work. They made her world-famous and extended her influence beyond Chicago. In 1907 she became a leader in the women's suffrage (right-to-vote) movement. In 1920, she helped found the American Civil Liberties Union, an organization that defends the rights and freedoms of people in the United States.

A lifelong supporter of peace, Addams strongly opposed World War I. She helped establish the Women's International League for Peace and Freedom and served as its president from 1919 until her death in 1935. Many people criticized her opposition to the war. The FBI called her "the most dangerous woman in America." But her work for world peace earned her the Nobel Peace Prize in 1931.

A century after its founding, the Henry Street Settlement on New York's Lower East Side still operates, offering a broad range of social and educational services.

The Settlement Movement

Jane Addams' impact on American life was enormous. Settlement houses modeled on Hull House were established in cities throughout the United States—Pillsbury House in Minneapolis, Grace Hill Neighborhood Center in St. Louis, Friendly House in Worcester, Massachusetts. Today there are over 800 neighborhood centers in the United States. They offer many services to the residents of their community, including day care, language classes, job training, and outreach programs.

Progressives in politics adopted many of the reforms Addams supported. They pressed for—and passed—new local, state, and national laws to protect women, children, and working people.

Jane Addams had encouraged young people, particularly women, to live and work among the poor. Her example inspired many women to choose careers in public service. A new professional field—social work—grew out of the settlement house movement and Addams' work at Hull House.

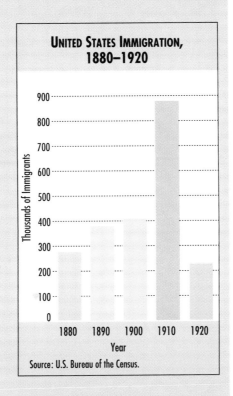

UNITED STATES IMMIGRATION, 1880–1920

Source: U.S. Bureau of the Census.

From 1880 to 1920, over two million immigrants came to the United States, creating an urgent need for assistance and reform.

Woodrow Wilson

As President of the United States, he tried to lead the world to a just and lasting peace after World War I.

The Era of Reform

By the turn of the 20th century, the United States had become an industrial giant. Millions of people had immigrated to America from Europe to work in its booming factories and mines. This rapid industrial and population growth caused many problems for the nation and its people. In the early 1900s, many groups urging various reforms joined the Progressive movement to fight corruption in government, curb the abuses of big business, and protect workers and consumers.

Woodrow Wilson, who would become an important Progressive leader, was born in 1856 in Staunton, Virginia. The son of a Presbyterian minister, he grew up with strong ideas about right and wrong. He became an uncompromising believer in equality and justice. Wilson served as president of Princeton University from 1907 to 1910 and as governor of New Jersey from 1910 to 1912. In each job, he was a reformer who achieved important changes.

President Wilson

Wilson was elected President of the United States in 1912. As President, he set out to reform the nation's business and financial affairs. Among his landmark reforms was a federal child labor law designed to protect children from having to work long hours in factories and mines. Wilson was also responsible for the first income tax—to make the wealthy pay their fair share of the nation's expenses. He established government agencies to oversee banking and to prevent unfair business practices.

Neutrality

War broke out in Europe in 1914, halfway through President Wilson's first term. The Allies—Great Britain, France, and Russia—were fighting against Germany and Austria-Hungary. In the United States, many people still had strong ties to their countries of origin in Europe. Most Americans, however, were isolationists. They preferred to remain uninvolved in the affairs of other nations—especially nations that were so far away. President Wilson officially proclaimed the country's neutrality and urged Americans not to take sides.

World War I

Wilson was reelected in 1916 on the slogan "He kept us out of war." He worked hard to make peace between the warring nations. He urged both sides to accept a

Wilson campaigned vigorously in the 1912 presidential election. His Progressive ideals and reputation as a reformer contributed to his victory.

"peace without victory," that is, to stop fighting and work out their differences at the negotiating table. Despite his efforts, the United States was drawn into the conflict when Germany sank U.S. ships. The nation entered the war in 1917 on the side of the Allies. U.S. troops, fighting alongside their war-weary allies, helped tip the balance of power in Europe.

The war ended with Germany's defeat in 1918. Millions of lives had been lost; homes and villages in Western Europe had been completely destroyed. President Wilson, hoping to prevent such devastation from occurring in the future, journeyed to Paris to help negotiate a peace treaty. Wilson received a hero's welcome. Thousands of French troops lined his route into Paris, and people all across Europe hailed him as "the champion of the rights of man."

Wilson brought to Paris a detailed plan for peace, his Fourteen Points. He wanted a peace based on "the eternal principles of right and justice," and he strongly disagreed with those who wanted to punish Germany. Most of all, he wanted to establish the League of Nations, an association of nations that would work together to maintain world peace.

Wilson was only partially successful in his peace efforts. The Allies, eager for revenge, imposed harsh penalties on Germany. During the months of negotiations, Wilson had to compromise on most of his Fourteen Points in order to get agreement on the League of Nations, which was established in 1920.

Organization for Peace

Wilson went home to campaign for public support for the League. He suffered a stroke while on a speaking tour in Colorado. The U.S. Senate refused to ratify the peace treaty and rejected the idea of membership in the League of Nations. Without U.S. backing, the League had little influence, though it lasted until the outbreak of World War II in 1939.

Despite the failure of his efforts, Wilson's ideas had a far-reaching effect. During World War II, the idea for an international peace organization was revived as the United Nations. This time the United States was a strong supporter and founding member of the organization. Today the UN continues its work to preserve world peace and to help nations work cooperatively to solve their problems.

Located in New York City, the United Nations is the realization of Wilson's idea for an organization to maintain world peace.

Once the United States entered the war, recruiting posters encouraged men to volunteer for the fight "to make the world safe for democracy."

I WANT YOU FOR U.S. ARMY
NEAREST RECRUITING STATION

Vladimir Ilich Lenin

After organizing and leading the Bolshevik Revolution, he created the first Communist state.

Discontent led to riots and the storming of the czar's palace. The Russian ruler and his family were forced to flee to safety.

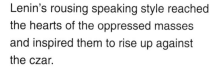

Lenin's rousing speaking style reached the hearts of the oppressed masses and inspired them to rise up against the czar.

Ready for Revolution

Russia was governed for hundreds of years by absolute rulers called czars. They allowed no political freedom and punished dissent harshly. From the 1880s on, Russia was a hotbed of revolution as various groups tried to overthrow the czar. At the beginning of the 20th century, Russia was still an underdeveloped agricultural society, though it had begun to develop industries and to build railroads. But the peasants were required to pay high taxes on their land, and factory workers labored long hours for very low wages.

Early in his life, Vladimir Ilich Lenin recognized the inequality in his country. He was born in 1870, the son of a middle-class government official. When Lenin was 17, his older brother was executed for plotting to assassinate Czar Alexander III. He studied law and became interested in the writings of Karl Marx and Friedrich Engels. These radical economic theorists predicted that the workers of the world would overthrow the factory owners and landlords. Then they would establish a socialist society in which business ownership and profits would be shared among all the people, not just a powerful few.

As a young man, Lenin became a Marxist revolutionary. He was arrested and spent three years imprisoned in Siberia. From 1900 to 1917, he lived in exile in Europe, where he maintained contact with Marxists in Russia and continued to call for revolution.

The Bolshevik Revolution

Early in the 20th century, Russia's peasants and workers grew more and more discontented. In addition, the people became increasingly frustrated and angry over their country's involvement in World War I and the government's inability to defeat the Germans.

When riots broke out in March 1917 over high food prices, the Russian Army joined the revolutionaries and forced Czar Nicholas II to abdicate. The Social Democrats, the moderate wing of the revolutionary party, established a provisional, or temporary, government to run the country until elections could be held.

The provisional government, led by Alexander Kerensky, promised the people an end to Russian participation in the war, land reform, and higher pay for the workers. However, government leaders, quarreling among themselves, were unable to keep those promises.

Lenin Seizes the Government In the meantime, Lenin, having returned to Russia, had become the leader of the Bolsheviks, the radical wing of the revolutionary party. He won popular support by promising the people "peace, land, and bread." In November 1917, the Bolsheviks took over the city of St. Petersburg, the national capital, and forced the Kerensky government from office.

The Bolsheviks established a committee of revolutionary rulers called the Council of People's Commissars. As chairman of the council, Lenin became, in effect, the ruler of all Russia.

The Bolsheviks soon changed their name to the Communist Party to reflect their belief in community ownership of property. Lenin sought to make Russia a socialist nation in which all factories, businesses, and farms were owned by the workers. Lenin believed that the workers would establish a worldwide "dictatorship of the proletariat," or working class, and that the nations of the world would "wither away." Russia remained a Communist Party dictatorship for more than seven decades.

The Failure of Communism

Lenin ruled the Communist Party until his death in 1924. During that time, a bloody civil war was fought between the Communists (the Reds) and various anti-Communist forces (the Whites). The civil war ended in 1921 with the Communists victorious, leaving the country in the grip of a severe famine. An estimated nine million people died from the war, disease, and starvation.

In 1922, Russia became the Union of Soviet Socialist Republics (USSR), a federation of Communist states stretching from Europe to the Pacific Ocean. The Communist Party grew in strength and influence. The leaders who followed Lenin continued to spread his dream of international Communist revolution around the world.

Few people thought that the powerful Communist system would ever weaken or that Communist ideas would cease to appeal to the world's poor. Thus, the collapse of communism in Eastern Europe in 1989 came as a tremendous shock. Even more shocking was the end of the Soviet Union itself, which came in December 1991 with the resignation of Mikhail Gorbachev.

After Lenin's death, the Communist Party raised him nearly to the level of a god. Over the years, millions of Soviet citizens viewed his body, which is on permanent display in Moscow.

Mohandas Gandhi

He challenged the power of the British Empire and achieved independence for India through nonviolent protest.

Colonial Rule Versus Civil Rights

Great Britain ruled the Indian subcontinent from the early 1700s until well into the 20th century. For much of that period, India was a troubled country. Britain did little to improve the lives of the Indian people. A rigid system of social classes, or castes, dominated Indian society. Religious conflict between the Hindu majority and the Muslim minority divided the nation.

Mohandas Gandhi was born in 1869, the youngest child in a large Hindu family of the merchant caste. As he grew up, his deeply religious mother instilled in him the Hindu principles of nonviolence, tolerance, and inner peace.

Gandhi earned a law degree in England and accepted a one-year contract to practice law in South Africa. There he had his first encounter with racial discrimination. He was beaten by whites, barred from a hotel, and thrown off a train during a trip to Pretoria. The experience changed Gandhi from a shy and retiring person to an outspoken advocate for the Indians of South Africa. He remained in South Africa for 20 years fighting for the rights of the Indians who lived there.

Gandhi Returns to India

After World War I, Indians began to demand independence for their country. Gandhi, who had returned to India in 1915, soon became the leader of the independence movement.

Gandhi believed that the independence movement should include all Indians, not just the wealthy and educated classes. To help break down the barriers between the castes, he lived among the untouchables, the lowest class, who were shunned by all the others. Next, he persuaded many people from all parts of India to form a nationwide democratic organization. The aim of this All-Indian Congress Committee was to negotiate with the British for India's independence.

Pacifist Leader Gandhi was as much a religious and spiritual leader as he was a political one. His followers called him Mahatma, which means "the great soul." He believed that nonviolence was the most moral and effective means of opposing the British. His nonviolent methods included strikes, marches, fasts, and boycotts of British businesses, goods, and institutions.

He urged Indians to practice civil disobedience, to refuse to obey unjust laws. He led hundreds of followers on a 200-mile march to the sea to make salt from salt water. This was to protest a tax on salt, a tax that mostly affected the poor. Although Gandhi and thousands of his followers were often imprisoned, they never resisted arrest, and they endured prison with quiet dignity.

Gandhi promoted self-reliance and pride in Indian-made products, by abandoning Western-style clothing.

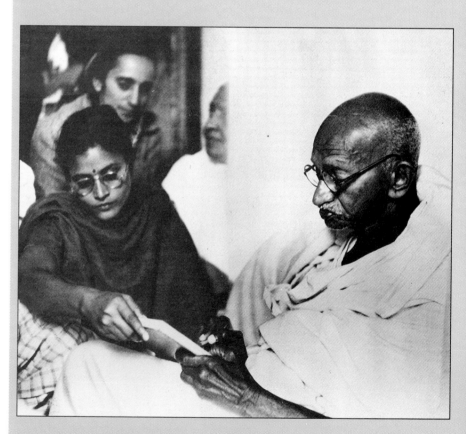

Gandhi's moral conviction, persuasive power, and just cause led millions to follow him.

He took to spinning cloth and wearing simple homemade garments. He often fasted, sometimes for weeks at a time, to protest the plight of the untouchables and British oppression, or to quell riots and violence among his followers.

A Divided Nation Gandhi worked hard to unite India's Hindu and Muslim factions and to establish religious tolerance. He was unable to achieve these goals. After India supported the British cause in World War II, Great Britain gave India its independence in 1947. However, unable to resolve the differences between the Muslims and the Hindus, Britain divided the country into two independent nations, Pakistan (Muslim) and India (Hindu). In 1971, the eastern part of Pakistan became Bangladesh.

Many groups, including the United Farm Workers in the United States, have adopted Gandhi's techniques of nonviolent protest to advance their causes.

Gandhi's Influence

Gandhi's death in 1948 sent shock waves throughout the world. On his way to an evening prayer meeting, Gandhi was assassinated by a young Hindu fanatic. He left behind one of the world's largest democracies, but he also left a troubled and divided nation.

In the years since independence, religious conflict has continued to plague India. It has experienced years of riots, mass migrations, terrorism, and repression. India's leaders have developed the nation into an industrial power. But they have never been able to stem its runaway population growth or overcome the extreme poverty of large segments of its population.

Gandhi's philosophy of nonviolent protest has left its mark on the rest of the world. Many independence and civil rights movements adopted his methods. In the United States, Martin Luther King, Jr., Cesar Chavez, and others have successfully used nonviolence to advance their causes.

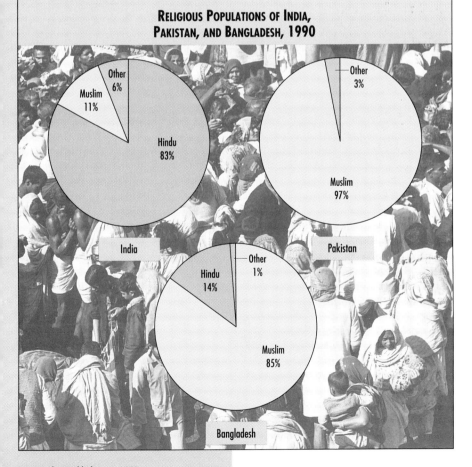

RELIGIOUS POPULATIONS OF INDIA, PAKISTAN, AND BANGLADESH, 1990

India: Other 6%, Muslim 11%, Hindu 83%

Pakistan: Other 3%, Muslim 97%

Bangladesh: Hindu 14%, Other 1%, Muslim 85%

Source: *The World Almanac,* 1992.

Gandhi's India is now divided into three separate nations. But tension among people of different religions still erupts into violence, as it did in India in 1992.

Adolf Hitler

◆

As dictator of Nazi Germany, he plunged the world into war and brought about the Holocaust.

Hitler reached the height of his career in 1941, when he controlled most of Europe and even a large part of the Soviet Union.

GERMAN EXPANSION IN EUROPE, 1939–1942

Under German Control in 1939 (prior to World War II)

Allied with Germany

Occupied by Germany

National Boundaries, 1939

• Cities

Hitler's passionate and compelling speaking style led Germany to war and to vicious crimes against humanity.

Rumblings of Discontent

Germany, defeated in World War I, was further humiliated by the terms of the peace treaty signed at Versailles in 1919. Germany was forced to reduce its armed forces and to pay huge reparations, or war damages, to the countries it had fought against. It did so to compensate them for their losses. The new democratic government was weak, and many Germans regarded it as a foreign system imposed by the victorious Allies—Britain, France, and the United States. A decade of runaway inflation, high unemployment, and political turmoil following the war left the nation ready for a strong leader who offered visions of a new German empire.

Adolf Hitler was born in Austria-Hungary in 1889. A drifter and an unsuccessful art student, he moved to Munich, Germany, and joined the army during World War I. After the war he joined the tiny German Workers' Party and molded it into the National Socialist (Nazi) Party. A powerful and mesmerizing speaker, Hitler called on Germans to follow their patriotic destiny and build a new and racially pure German empire. Hitler attempted to seize power in Munich in 1923 but was arrested and imprisoned. In prison, Hitler wrote *Mein Kampf* ("My Struggle"). The book, in which he described his life and political ideas, became the bible of the Nazi movement.

German soldiers rounded up Jewish families to send them to concentration camps, where they were killed. This was Hitler's "final solution."

Hitler's Rise to Power

In 1929, Germany was hit hard by the Great Depression. Foreign countries demanded payment of the loans that were helping the country rebuild after the war. Factories were forced to close, and millions of Germans were left unemployed.

After his release from prison, Hitler worked to strengthen the Nazi Party. By 1932, the party had won enough votes in the national elections to enable Hitler to become chancellor. One of his first acts was to give himself dictatorial powers. Hitler called his government the Third Reich (empire) and took the title Führer, meaning "leader."

Hitler fiercely hated the Jews, blaming them for Germany's ills. With his secret police, called the Gestapo, and his storm troopers, Hitler began to wage a war against the Jews. He deprived them of their rights as citizens and drove them from their jobs. During *Kristallnacht,* the "night of broken glass," in November 1938, rampaging gangs and storm troopers smashed Jewish homes and shops, killing, beating, and terrorizing Jews across the country. Many Jews were sent to concentration camps.

World War II Hitler's ambitions grew beyond the borders of Germany. He defied the Treaty of Versailles and rebuilt the German Army. In 1939, he launched a war, invading his European neighbors—Poland, Belgium, and France. By 1941, Germany was involved in a second world war against the Allies—Britain, France, the Soviet Union, and the United States. By 1942, Germany had conquered or controlled most of Europe.

As the war progressed, Hitler devised his "final solution" for what he called "the Jewish problem." Jews from all parts of German-controlled Europe, especially from Eastern Europe, were sent to concentration camps, where they were systematically murdered. Hitler's Nazis killed six million European Jews, as well as an estimated five million other persons of various faiths and nationalities. This is remembered as the Holocaust.

In 1945, Germany was again defeated in a world war. Facing unconditional surrender, Hitler committed suicide in his bunker in Berlin. His "thousand-year Reich" dissolved in the rubble that was left behind by Allied bombings.

Europe Divided

The war Hitler waged and lost brought profound changes to the world. As many as 50 million people died in the war, and Europe was left devastated. Western Europe was rebuilt, in part through the help of the United States in a program called the Marshall Plan.

The Soviet Union established control over Eastern Europe, where it imposed Communist governments on eight nations. One of those nations was East Germany. Hitler's Reich had been divided into two countries— East Germany and West Germany. West Germany became allied with the United States. The two Germanys stood in conflict, part of the struggle between the United States and the Soviet Union called the Cold War. The two parts were not united until 1990, when the Cold War ended.

The once thriving Jewish civilization of Europe was destroyed. Many of the Jews who survived emigrated to Palestine, where they helped to establish the new state of Israel in 1948.

A new generation of right wing radicals has begun harassing foreigners in Germany. In 1992, neo-Nazi youths firebombed several homes where foreigners live, killing three Turkish immigrants and injuring others.

13

Winston Churchill

◆

As British prime minister, he rallied the nation to resist the Nazis during World War II.

The Failure of Appeasement

In 1938, Prime Minister Neville Chamberlain of Great Britain and the leaders of France and Italy met in Munich with Adolf Hitler, the Nazi dictator, to discuss the problem of Czechoslovakia. Hitler had made many aggressive moves on the pretext of reclaiming German territory lost in World War I. Britain and other nations watched, but did nothing, until 1938. Then Hitler moved to take the Sudetenland, a part of Czechoslovakia where Germans lived. At the Munich meeting, a deal was made. Hitler could have the Sudetenland in exchange for his promise to halt any further aggression.

Chamberlain believed in a policy of appeasement. He felt that by giving Hitler what he wanted, Hitler would be satisfied and peace would be preserved. Winston Churchill, however, tried to warn the world against Hitler.

The Munich agreement, he said, was "a disaster of the first magnitude," and he was right. Hitler had no intention of stopping with the Sudetenland.

Winston Churchill, born in 1874, was the son of an upper-class Conservative politician. After graduating from the Royal Military College at Sandhurst, he was hired as a war correspondent to cover conflicts in Cuba and South Africa. In South Africa, Churchill was captured and imprisoned by the Boers, descendants of Dutch settlers in South Africa who were fighting the British. He escaped by scaling the prison wall, evading the sentries, and traveling more than 300 miles on freight trains through enemy territory. The news of his daring escape turned him into a hero.

Churchill chose a career in politics and was elected to Parliament in 1900 as a member of the Conservative, or Tory, Party. He was appointed to the position of first lord of the admiralty in 1911 and ably commanded the British Navy during World War I. After the war, he served in various government posts, including secretary of war, chancellor of the exchequer (treasury), and head of the colonial office. As a politician, Churchill was a man of enormous energy who threw himself wholeheartedly into every issue. In 1929 he fell out of favor and left government service for ten years.

Churchill shows his trademark "V for victory" sign. His ability to inspire the British people helped his nation survive the war.

> "... we shall defend our island, whatever the cost may be. We shall fight on the beaches, we shall fight on the landing grounds, we shall fight in the fields and in the streets, we shall fight in the hills; we shall never surrender."

▲ In this excerpt from a radio speech, June 4, 1940, Churchill expressed the British resolve to fight the Germans.

▶ Churchill surveys the damage caused by German bombs during the Blitz.

Wartime Leader

After Britain declared war on Germany in 1939, Churchill was reassigned to his former post as first lord of the admiralty. When Chamberlain resigned as prime minister a year later, Churchill was chosen to succeed him. Faced with the threat of a German invasion, Churchill immediately began organizing the defense of Britain. He mobilized troops and converted factories to weapons production. Most importantly, he inspired the people to resist German aggression. "Victory at all costs," he proclaimed, "victory in spite of all terror, victory however long and hard the road may be; for without victory there is no survival."

The Blitz When Hitler launched the Blitz, a fierce air war against Britain, the Royal Air Force fought back heroically. Churchill, a man of great personal courage, was frequently seen observing the air battles. He toured bomb-damaged areas in London and throughout Britain, giving his famous "V for victory" sign to rally the people.

The Grand Alliance In 1940, Churchill met with President Franklin Roosevelt. Although the United States was not yet in the war, Roosevelt provided aid to Britain. The following year marked a turning point in the war. Hitler suddenly turned against his allies and invaded the USSR. The Japanese attack on Pearl Harbor and Hitler's declaration of war against the United States brought America into the conflict. Churchill lost no time in forging an alliance with these two nations against their common enemy—Hitler. Churchill was always an unswerving opponent of communism and greatly distrusted the Soviet leader, Joseph Stalin. But he forced himself to work with him for the sake of the war effort. Churchill, Stalin, and an American president met three times—in Tehran (Iran), Yalta (Russia), and Potsdam (Germany). They worked out military strategy and planned for the disarmament and occupation of Germany after the war. They also negotiated peace treaties with Germany and the occupied countries of Europe and laid the foundations for a new international peace organization, the United Nations.

The Coming of the Cold War

Churchill's last meeting with Stalin and an American president—Harry Truman, now that Roosevelt had died—took place in Potsdam in July 1945. Before the conference ended, Churchill's party lost the parliamentary election and he was replaced as prime minister. He returned home and became the opposition leader in the House of Commons.

Just as he had warned the world against Hitler, Churchill was also the first to denounce Soviet expansion after the war had ended. In a 1946 speech in Fulton, Missouri, Churchill charged that the Soviet Union had dropped "an iron curtain" across Europe. He warned of the coming Cold War between the USSR and the Western democracies.

Churchill served once more as prime minister, between 1951 and 1955, and remained in Parliament nearly until his death in 1965 at the age of 90. He is remembered and revered even today for his crucial role in saving Britain during its darkest hour.

Franklin Delano Roosevelt

◆

As President, he brought the United States out of the Great Depression and guided it through World War II.

Roosevelt's confident air gave hope to Americans during the dark days of the Great Depression and World War II.

Widespread unemployment, poverty, and hunger forced thousands of Americans to stand in breadlines for free food.

Economic Collapse: Enter Roosevelt

When Herbert Hoover was elected president in 1928, the United States was in a period of prosperity and growth. Those good times ended one year later when prices on the stock market fell dramatically. This stock market crash became a symbol of the economic collapse called the Great Depression. The results were disastrous:

- Over 100,000 businesses closed.
- Nearly 15 million people lost their jobs.
- Banks collapsed, wiping out people's life savings.
- Farmers lost their land and families their homes.

Blaming Hoover for their plight, the American people elected Franklin Delano Roosevelt in 1932.

Born into a wealthy New York family, Roosevelt attended Harvard University. In 1905, he married Anna Eleanor Roosevelt, the niece of former President Theodore Roosevelt. Despite being crippled by polio in 1921, Roosevelt was a confident and energetic man.

Roosevelt's Presidency

During the presidential campaign of 1932, Roosevelt had promised Americans a "New Deal"—a plan for national economic recovery. Upon taking office, he called Congress into special session for 100 days to enact New Deal programs.

The New Deal Roosevelt created new government agencies to regulate business and protect workers. The New Deal programs included the following:

- The Rural Electrification Administration, which made electric power available to farmers.
- The Social Security Act, which gave pensions to the elderly and disabled.
- The Civilian Conservation Corps, which created jobs to build irrigation systems and conserve farmland.
- The Works Progress Administration, which provided jobs building roads, schools, dams, and airports.
- The National Labor Relations Act, which gave workers the right to join labor unions.

President Roosevelt's swift action and confident manner reassured

many Americans. His radio addresses to the nation, which he called "fireside chats," lifted people's spirits. Working-class Americans adored Roosevelt. Conservative Republican voters and a majority of business leaders, however, opposed the President. They felt that he had gone too far in making the government responsible for the welfare of the people.

World War II Despite Roosevelt's efforts, the nation did not fully recover from the Great Depression until it began to prepare for World War II. Americans watched with indifference during the 1930s as a major conflict developed in Europe. Most people in the United States felt that the nation should stay out of overseas affairs.

In 1940, Roosevelt was elected to an unprecedented third term as President. He recognized the need to prepare for America's possible entry in the war. He began a massive military buildup and established the first peacetime draft. In 1941, Roosevelt and British prime minister Winston Churchill signed the Atlantic Charter, which stated the postwar aims of their two nations. The United States also agreed to provide aid to Britain.

The United States entered the war at the end of 1941, after the Japanese bombed the U.S. naval base at Pearl Harbor. Throughout the war, Roosevelt traveled across the nation to keep morale high. He met with Stalin and Churchill to coordinate the war effort. His courage, energy, and optimism helped rally the American people.

In 1945, Roosevelt planned to attend a 50-nation conference to draft the charter for the United Nations. However, his health had been failing for some time. He collapsed and died on April 12, just two weeks before the conference and only a few months before the end of the war.

After Roosevelt

Millions of people in the United States still benefit from the programs, such as Social Security, that Roosevelt established in the 1930s. His New Deal marked a major change in government policy. His new idea was that the federal government should be responsible for those who need help—poor, elderly, homeless, or unemployed people. The New Deal led to the enormous growth of government as new agencies and departments were created to administer the programs.

Roosevelt's leadership during World War II helped to turn America away from isolationism. With the war and its aftermath, the United States and the Soviet Union became major rivals for world power—a rivalry that lasted nearly five decades.

The construction of this dam and the painting of the mural depicting it were both funded by the WPA, which put three million people to work.

Joseph Stalin

The Soviet dictator made his country a great industrial and military power, but at a frightful cost to the people he ruled.

By systematically eliminating those who opposed him, Stalin became the absolute ruler of the Soviet Union.

Man of Steel

Czar Alexander III ruled Russia in 1879, the year of Joseph Stalin's birth. Like the czars before him, Alexander governed with an iron fist, allowing no political freedom.

Stalin's father, a cruel man who often beat his son, died when Joseph was ten. His mother sent him to a religious school to train for the priesthood. There Stalin secretly read Karl Marx, a political and economic theorist who called for the overthrow of the ruling class and the establishment of a socialist, worker-controlled state. In 1899, Stalin was expelled from school for revolutionary activities. He joined a group of political radicals in his native Georgia.

Between 1901 and 1917 Stalin was exiled to Siberia seven times for revolutionary activities. Eventually he became a follower of Vladimir Ilich Lenin, the leader of the Bolsheviks, the socialist group that would seize power in 1917.

Born Iosif V. Dzhugashvili, Stalin lived and worked under several names. In 1913 he adopted the one that stuck: Stalin, which meant "man of steel." It fit him. He was strong-willed and ambitious, often ruthless in his quest for power.

Stalin's Rise to Power

When the Bolsheviks seized control of the Russian government in 1917, Lenin became the country's leader. The Bolsheviks now called themselves Communists. Stalin was appointed to the post of general secretary of the Communist Party, a position of enormous power. As general secretary, Stalin was responsible for assigning people to government jobs. He made sure to place his supporters in positions where they could help him most.

Lenin's death in 1924 set off a fierce power struggle between Stalin and his main rival, Leon Trotsky. Stalin won in part because of the power he had gained as general secretary, and in part by exaggerating the closeness of his relationship with Lenin. After he took control, Stalin forced Trotsky into exile and later had him assassinated.

Plans for Development When Stalin took over the Communist Party and the government of Russia, he instituted the first of a series of five-year plans to increase the country's industrial power and raise factory production. At the same time, he forced Russia's farmers to pool their

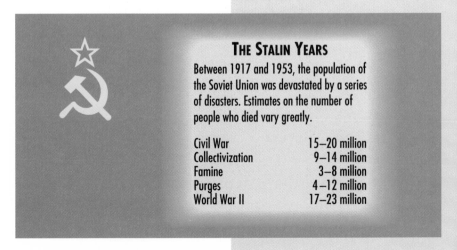

THE STALIN YEARS
Between 1917 and 1953, the population of the Soviet Union was devastated by a series of disasters. Estimates on the number of people who died vary greatly.

Civil War	15–20 million
Collectivization	9–14 million
Famine	3–8 million
Purges	4–12 million
World War II	17–23 million

livestock and land into collective farms where everything was owned jointly. When farmers resisted—as many did—Stalin sent them to labor camps or had them killed. Many millions of Russian peasants are thought to have died from starvation, imprisonment, or execution during these years.

Throughout the 1930s, Stalin engaged in a massive reign of terror known as the purges. His aim was to strengthen his control of the party and the government. Stalin had almost all of the original Bolsheviks removed by accusing them of various charges, trying them, and executing them. He rounded up millions of government officials, teachers, artists, military officers, and others who he believed were disloyal to him. Some were executed. Many more were sent to labor camps in Siberia, where most of them died.

World War II In 1939, Stalin signed a treaty with Adolf Hitler, the German leader. They agreed not to attack each other and to divide Poland between them. But after Germany attacked Russia in 1941, Stalin joined the effort to defeat Hitler. The Soviet people endured severe hardships during the war; millions died from starvation and disease. Stalin's annexation of Poland, Latvia, Lithuania, and Estonia forced millions of people to accept Communist rule. However, his leadership did help the nation survive and defeat the Nazis.

After the war, Stalin's determination to impose communism on Eastern Europe brought him into conflict with Western Europe and the United States. By 1948, the conflict escalated into global confrontation between the forces of communism and the forces of democracy. This confrontation became known as the Cold War.

Stalin's Influence

Stalin's chief legacy to the world was fear. No other Soviet leader ever wielded so much personal power. He was a totalitarian ruler, a cruel and ruthless man who killed tens of millions of his own people. Still many Russians honored him for saving the nation during World War II, modernizing it, and turning it into an industrial power. He centralized the Soviet economic, political, and social systems. In so doing, he created an enormous bureaucracy that controlled every aspect of life in the Soviet Union. While Stalin's economic policies officially eliminated unemployment, they also robbed workers of any incentive to work hard.

The Cold War, begun during Stalin's reign, resulted in an arms race in which both Communist and democratic nations built huge stockpiles of nuclear missiles and other weapons.

After Stalin died in 1953, his successor, Nikita Khrushchev, denounced him and attempted to reform the dictatorial state and the Communist Party he had inherited from Stalin. Even today—four decades after his death and several years after the collapse of the Soviet Union—Stalin's memory inspires both admiration and condemnation.

Churchill (*left*), Roosevelt (*center*), and Stalin met at Yalta. Decisions made there and afterward set the course for the Cold War that followed World War II.

Mao Zedong

As a revolutionary leader, he modernized the world's most populous nation.

The End of Dynastic Rule

Mao Zedong (Mao Tse-Tung) was born in 1893 into a China that had been ruled by emperors and hereditary dynasties for centuries. In Mao's youth, the ruling Manchu dynasty was weak, and the country was dominated by fierce warlords and populated by millions of poor peasants. The Manchu rulers wanted to keep China closed off from the rest of the world. But the Manchu government was too weak to prevent the United States, Russia, France, Germany, and Japan from establishing colonies in China. At the same time, Chinese students, under the leadership of Sun Yat-sen, formed revolutionary groups. When they finally overthrew the Manchus in 1911, Sun established a republic, but it, too, was weak. The country was in a constant state of turmoil as the warlords competed for power.

Mao had played a minor part in the 1911 revolution. At the same time that he became an official of the new government, Mao, a Marxist, secretly began organizing the Chinese Communist Party.

Mao's Rise to Power

Sun Yat-sen tried to establish order through his nationalist party, the Kuomintang. When he died in 1925, the party was taken over by Jiang Jie-shi (Chiang Kai-shek), a Kuomintang army officer. Meanwhile, Mao planned ways to adapt the Communist revolution to China. Instead of recruiting party members from among industrial workers, as had been done in other countries, Mao decided to gather followers from among China's millions of poor peasants.

Civil War When Jiang Jie-shi turned against the Communist Party and the peasantry in 1927, Mao formed the Red Army and retreated to the countryside in southeastern China. That step began a 22-year-long civil war against the Nationalists. In 1934, Mao and his followers were forced to flee their stronghold in Hunan Province and retreat to Yenan in northwest China. It was during this legendary Long March—a trek of 5,000 miles—that Mao consolidated, or united, his power and became the supreme leader of the Chinese Communists.

The Chinese civil war was temporarily halted in 1937 when the Communist and Nationalist forces joined to fight the Japanese, who had invaded Manchuria. Throughout the war years that followed, however, Mao never stopped building his army or organizing the peasants. When the Japanese were defeated in 1945, the civil war resumed and lasted for four more years. In 1949, Mao's forces drove the Nationalists from mainland China to the island of Taiwan. In Beijing, Mao established the People's Republic of China with himself as premier.

Mao, shown here on horseback during the Long March, led the Communists to victory in China. His writings inspired Marxist revolutionaries throughout the world.

The Great Leap Forward In the early years of his regime, Mao destroyed China's ancient class system by executing or imprisoning hundreds of thousands of upper-class capitalists and landlords. Then he set out to transform China's backward economy by "the Great Leap Forward." Basing the new economic system on the Soviet model, he

- brought business and industry under state control;
- established thousands of collective farms;
- organized workers into communes—efficient work units that were assigned to work in factories and fields.

The communes had kitchens, schools, and nurseries to free the women to work alongside the men. Mao also employed Soviet-style five-year plans, goals for boosting industrial production. The results were mixed. Some industrial progress was made, but collectivization of agriculture produced widespread famine and millions of deaths.

The Cultural Revolution In the early years, Mao had forged close ties with the Soviet Union. But by 1960, he had split with the Soviet leaders. By the mid-1960s, Mao had become convinced that China's aging Communist leaders had become too privileged. He purged the party of its senior officials and urged young people to rebel against their elders. This so-called Cultural Revolution, which lasted several years, resulted in the beating, imprisonment, and death of tens of thousands of doctors, teachers, and other professionals. Another result of Mao's split with the Soviet Union was that it pushed him toward friendship with the Soviet Union's chief superpower rival, the United States.

Mao's Impact

By the time of his death in 1976, Mao had already been recognized as the most important revolutionary and nationalist leader of the Third World. His writings were widely published throughout the world. They became an instruction manual for Marxist revolution in dozens of countries in Asia, Africa, and South America.

Mao's impact on China was profound. He established China's sovereignty as an independent nation after years of colonial rule by foreign powers. He transformed the nation from a backward agricultural society to one of the world's industrial powers. The Cultural Revolution, however, had long-term and negative effects, which included the continued use of force to suppress opposition. Unlike the Soviet Union, communism has survived in China. But it no longer commands the loyalty of much of the population. In 1989, student protests escalated into a popular prodemocracy movement in Beijing and 20 other cities. Thousands of students and workers were killed or injured; thousands more were arrested.

Major Events in Modern Chinese History

1911	Sun Yat-sen overthrows Manchus and establishes republic.
1920	Chinese Communist Party is founded by Mao Zedong and others.
1927	Civil war begins between the Nationalists and the Chinese Communists.
1937	Japan invades China. Nationalists and Communists temporarily unite to fight the Japanese.
1949	Mao establishes People's Republic of China.
1966	The Cultural Revolution purges party officials, doctors, teachers, and others.
1989	Chinese students demonstrate for political reforms in Tiananmen Square. Rebellion is crushed by Chinese army.

In 1966, millions of young Chinese formed the Red Guards. Their mission was to root out those who had "taken the capitalist road." The result was years of upheaval and devastation.

21

Ho Chi Minh

As the leader of Vietnam, he ended colonial control of his country after World War II.

"We hold the truth that all men are created equal, that they are endowed by their creator with certain unalienable rights, among them life, liberty, and the pursuit of happiness."

On September 2, 1945, Ho Chi Minh declared Vietnam's independence. Borrowing from America's Declaration of Independence, Ho emphasized his strong belief in basic human rights.

French Rule in Asia

Vietnam is a small country in Southeast Asia, just south of China. It had endured a long history of civil wars, occupations, and dynastic rulers by the time the French took it as a colony in the 1700s. By 1887, France had combined Vietnam, Laos, and Cambodia into one large colony, the Indo-Chinese Union. From the turn of the century until World War II, various Vietnamese nationalist groups attempted to oust the French. But they all failed.

The man who was able to eventually achieve independence, Ho Chi Minh, was born Nguyen That Thanh in northern Vietnam in 1890. His father was an anti-French nationalist.

Little is known about Ho's early life. He was a secretive man who engaged in many underground activities and used several aliases, or false names. It is known that in 1911, Ho took a job on a French ocean liner. That began a 30-year self-imposed exile from Vietnam while he honed his skills as a Marxist revolutionary.

By the end of World War I, he was living in Paris. There he tried to press the case for Vietnamese civil rights at the Versailles peace conference. His pleas did not succeed. Over the next two decades, Ho spent time in both Russia and China studying communism. At this time he also founded the Indo-Chinese Communist Party.

The Struggle for Independence

By 1941, the Japanese had occupied Indochina and had executed or imprisoned most of its French colonial administrators. That same year the Comintern (the worldwide organization of Communist parties) sent Ho Chi Minh to Vietnam to establish a Communist organization within the country. Ho formed a guerrilla force made up of nationalists and Communists, which he called the League for the Independence of Vietnam, or the Vietminh. Throughout the rest of the war, the Vietminh led the resistance against the Japanese in northern Vietnam. At the same time, other nationalists in the South tried to gain

Vietnamese independence by cooperating with the Japanese. It was during this period that Ho adopted the name Ho Chi Minh, which means "he who enlightens."

Democratic Republic Immediately following the war, the Vietminh launched a rebellion against the war-weary French. They quickly conquered much of northern Vietnam. Ho established the Democratic Republic of Vietnam, with himself as president, in the northern city of Hanoi. France continued to send more and more forces to fight the Vietminh. Nine years of war ended with France's decisive defeat in 1954 at Dien Bien Phu.

The Vietminh and French negotiated a settlement that was supposed to temporarily divide Vietnam into two territories—the Communist North and the French-controlled South—until elections could be held to unify the country. Those elections were never held, however. The southern half of Vietnam became a separate anti-Communist, military state with its capital in Saigon.

U.S. Involvement From the outset, Ho Chi Minh wanted to reunite the North and the South. The new government of South Vietnam enjoyed the strong backing of the United States. But it was too weak to prevent the invasion of North Vietnamese forces and strikes by the Vietcong, Communist guerrillas living in the South. Although the United States sent hundreds of thousands of troops to South Vietnam, it was unable to defeat Ho's forces. In 1968, the Vietcong launched a costly all-out attack, the Tet Offensive. Although the Vietcong and the North Vietnamese lost thousands of soldiers, they fought the army of the world's most powerful nation—the United States—to a standstill. Ho Chi Minh died in 1969, but his successors carried the war to a successful conclusion.

In the United States, the Vietnam War grew more and more unpopular. In the early 1970s, the United States gradually pulled its troops out of South Vietnam, leaving that nation to fight on alone. The war ended when Saigon fell to the North Vietnamese in 1975. The two countries were reunited as the Socialist Republic of Vietnam.

During years of war and suffering, thousands of Vietnamese people were forced to flee their war-torn villages.

Aftermath of War

To millions of Vietnamese, Ho Chi Minh was "Uncle Ho," the very symbol of Vietnamese nationalism. He was not, however, a kindly uncle. His Communist regime in North Vietnam was very repressive. It treated the South Vietnamese people harshly after the war, forcing thousands to flee the country. Later most of those refugees were resettled in the United States and other countries.

Ho's successors have struggled since the 1970s to rebuild Vietnam's war-ravaged economy with mixed results. The new nation has remained isolated from much of the world. Today, Ho's lifelong dream of a unified, independent Vietnam is a reality, but its people remain in poverty and oppressed. Continued controversy over Americans missing in action has prevented the United States from sending aid to Vietnam.

23

Gamal Abdel Nasser

◆

A strong nationalist, he freed Egypt from foreign rule and restored dignity and pride to the Arab world.

Control of the Suez Canal

Great Britain controlled Egypt for 70 years, from 1882 until 1952. During that period, Egypt remained a poor and overpopulated nation of landless peasants and poor farmers. In 1922, the British permitted Egypt a small measure of independence. Although Egypt established a constitutional monarchy, Great Britain was the power behind the new throne.

Egypt was crucial to the vast British Empire. As long as Britain occupied Egypt, it retained control of the Suez Canal. The canal was the shortest shipping route between Europe and the Indian Ocean.

Gamal Abdel Nasser was born in Alexandria, Egypt, in 1918. Even as a schoolboy, he hated the British. He was known to have taken part in several anti-British street demonstrations. After graduating from the Royal Military Academy, Nasser served in the Egyptian Army. There he and three other army officers formed a secret revolutionary society, the Free Officers Committee. Their aim was to overthrow the British and the Egyptian royal family.

Nasser's Rule

By 1952, the committee had grown. On July 23, Nasser and 89 other Free Officers staged a nearly bloodless coup ousting Britain's puppet monarch, King Farouk. The officers established a military government. Nasser became prime minister in 1954 and president in 1956. During his early years in office, Nasser wrote the Egyptian constitution. He concentrated on developing the nation's economy and improving the lives of the peasants. One of his first actions was to redistribute land, taking it from the wealthy and giving it to the poor. Nasser also forced Great Britain to withdraw its troops from the Suez Canal Zone.

The United Arab Republic Nasser was widely admired by many Arabs, both in Egypt and in neighboring countries. He was the first Arab leader to establish a modern

Although Nasser tried to modernize Egyptian agriculture, most farmers still use traditional methods.

When the floodgates are opened, water from the Nile River comes through the Aswan Dam, producing electric power for much of Egypt.

Arab society. He campaigned vigorously against political corruption and expanded the legal rights of women. Nasser was also admired for his efforts to unite the Arab world. In 1958, he formed the United Arab Republic (UAR) with Syria. Nasser hoped the UAR would eventually include the entire Arab world. But the union never grew and lasted only three years.

The Aswan High Dam One of Nasser's most important achievements was the construction of the Aswan High Dam. The dam spurred industrial growth and brought electrical power to much of rural Egypt. When the United States and Great Britain backed out of their offers to finance the dam project, Nasser seized the Suez Canal. He planned to use tolls from the canal to finance the dam. His action prompted Israel, France, and Britain to invade Egypt in October 1956. Israel occupied the

Sinai Peninsula. The French and British attacked Egyptian airfields, destroying the Egyptian Air Force. The United States, however, forced these countries to retreat and negotiated an agreement leaving the canal in Egypt's hands. The United States hoped that its pro-Egyptian actions would persuade Nasser not to ally his nation with the Soviet Union. Nasser became a great hero throughout the Arab world.

The Six-Day War Despite American intervention, Nasser formed close ties with the Soviet Union, which provided money to finish the dam. Nasser also rebuilt Egypt's military forces, purchasing arms from another Communist country, Czechoslovakia. In 1967, after Egypt closed the Gulf of Aqaba to Israeli ships, Israel successfully attacked Egypt. Israel won the war in just six days. Nasser was so badly humiliated by that loss that he offered to resign. He remained in office, however, until 1970, when he died suddenly of a heart attack.

A Limited Success

Nasser freed Egypt from British rule and established an independent Arab nation. As a result, he restored pride and dignity to millions of Arabs who had lived under foreign dominations for centuries. He enjoyed enormous personal popularity. He did not, however, succeed in uniting the Arab world.

Nasser modernized Egypt to a great extent. Yet he was unable to eliminate the poverty in which most Egyptians lived. His continued refusal to recognize Israel forced him to channel much of the country's resources into weapons and disastrous wars instead of into domestic economic programs.

Nasser was succeeded by Anwar Sadat, one of the Free Officers who had participated in the 1952 coup. Sadat rid the country of Soviet military advisers and was the first Arab leader to recognize and make peace with Israel—a peace that has continued to last.

Israeli soldiers fight at night during the 1967 war. Tension between Israel and the Arab states still lingers.

Nasser's charismatic leadership brought renewed pride to Egypt and the Arab world.

Jomo Kenyatta

He led Kenya through its struggle for independence and became the new nation's first president.

Kenyatta's strong and effective leadership of Kenya became a symbol for all of Africa.

British Colony in Africa

In 1895, a year after the birth of Jomo Kenyatta, Kenya came under British control. The country was named British East Africa, and the government of Great Britain encouraged British citizens to settle there. When Kenyatta was still a small boy learning to hunt and farm in his native village, the British built a railroad across the colony, opening the interior lands to European settlement. Soon Europeans owned large coffee plantations throughout the colony. Asians became its shopkeepers and business owners. The only jobs for black Africans in the thriving colony were as laborers or farm workers.

Jomo Kenyatta's family belonged to the Kikuyu, the largest ethnic group in Kenya. The Kikuyu lived mainly in the fertile highlands of west central Kenya. Then European settlers took away their land. When Kenyatta was a teenager, he left home to study at a Christian mission. From the mission school, he went to England to complete his education. He returned to Kenya to take a government job in Nairobi, the capital. There he became a prominent leader of the Kenyan movement for national independence. Kenyatta went to London in 1929 to lobby for Kikuyu land rights in the highlands. He remained in England for several years, studying at the London School of Economics and continuing his work for Kenyan independence.

The challenge that remains for Kenya, and much of Africa, is forging a modern society in the midst of many different traditional cultures.

Kenyatta's Rise to Power

When Kenyatta returned to Kenya in 1946, he was elected president of the newly formed Kenya African Union (KAU), a political action group. For the next six years he worked to reform Britain's colonial policies. Among Kenyatta's demands were the return of tribal lands, better educational opportunities for Africans, and African representation in the nation's government.

Then in 1952, a violent nationalist faction, the Mau Mau, went on a rampage. They savagely killed white settlers. Kenyatta was arrested and convicted of directing the violence. He always denied the charge, and many people believe he was unjustly convicted. Nevertheless, the British court sentenced him to seven years in prison and two more in exile. His reputation as a leader of Africa's anticolonial movement continued to grow.

Bowing to anticolonial pressure, the British gradually began to give up control of the government. Kenyatta had a major role in negotiating the

terms of Kenya's independence. The nationalists were allowed to form a political party, the Kenya African National Union (KANU). Kenyatta became its president while he was still in prison. When the country was granted its independence in 1963, KANU won the first free elections in the country by an overwhelming majority. Kenyatta was installed as Kenya's president, a post he held until his death in 1978.

Changing Kenya Under Kenyatta's leadership, Kenya developed a stable republican form of government under a president. Kenya also developed a capitalist economy that attracted many foreign investors. Agriculture, tourism, and industry all prospered. Kenyatta banned all racial discrimination between whites and blacks. As a result, thousands of Kenya's white settlers remained in the country after the nation became independent.

Unlike many other Third World nationalists, Kenyatta never embraced communism. He felt it was another form of colonialism. He did not align Kenya with either the Western democracies or the Communist bloc, but he always maintained close ties with the Western nations.

A new constitution, drawn up shortly after independence, gave Kenyans more personal freedom than they had had under British rule. Although politics were dominated by the Africans because they were by far the majority in the population, Asian and European citizens also participated. In 1969, however, a popular government official was assassinated. This led to a split between Kenyatta and his vice-president and the banning of the opposition Kenya People's Party.

After Kenyatta

Jomo Kenyatta died in 1978. He was a popular and widely admired leader. Kenyatta inspired Africans in other countries to work for national independence and human rights. And he demonstrated that independence could be achieved without civil war or violence.

Kenyatta was succeeded by Daniel arap Moi. Moi continued the social and economic programs that had been started by Kenyatta. But he also tightened KANU's grip on the government. He changed Kenya's constitution to legalize one-party rule.

In December 1992, Kenya held the first multiparty election in 26 years. Despite charges of violence against the opposition and widespread voting irregularities, Daniel arap Moi was declared the winner.

The nation's economy made much progress under Kenyatta's leadership. Tourism is one of the most important industries in Kenya (*graph*). Safaris are a popular tourist attraction.

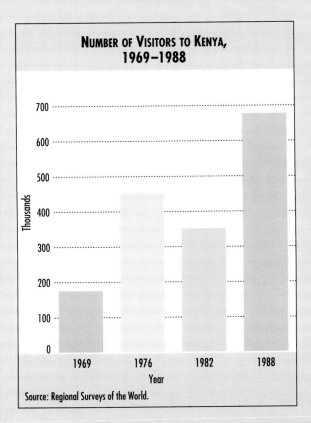

NUMBER OF VISITORS TO KENYA, 1969–1988

(Thousands; Year)

Source: Regional Surveys of the World.

Fidel Castro

His revolution overthrew a dictator and turned Cuba into Latin America's first and longest-lasting Communist state.

Castro (*center*) led his revolution from Cuba's eastern mountains. Eventually, his small band of guerrilla fighters toppled the Batista regime.

Opposing a Dictator

The United States had freed Cuba from Spanish control in the Spanish-American War at the turn of the century. For 50 years, Cuba struggled to become a stable democracy. It depended heavily on economic aid from the United States, which maintained naval bases on the island and periodically intervened in Cuban politics. Fulgencio Batista was in charge of Cuba from 1933 to 1959. He was a repressive, corrupt dictator who enjoyed close ties with the United States.

Many Cubans opposed Batista. One of them, Fidel Castro, would become the leader who succeeded in ousting the dictator. Castro was born in Oriente Province in 1926 and entered the University of Havana in 1945 to study law. Like so many rebels, Castro first became involved in revolutionary activities as a college student. His early revolutionary activities occurred outside Cuba—in the Dominican Republic in 1947 and in Colombia in 1948.

Castro in Command

By the 1950s, Castro had joined one of several revolutionary groups that had organized to depose Batista. In 1953, he led about 160 followers in a disastrous attack against an army barracks. Most were killed; many were captured. Castro himself was imprisoned until 1955, when he was released in a general amnesty. Castro fled to Mexico, where he built a new military force to continue guerrilla warfare against Batista. He returned to Cuba in 1956 with a force of 83 men. All but 12 were soon killed or captured. The survivors fled to the Sierra Maestra mountains.

Castro then began to attract new followers and to wage a guerrilla war against government troops. Within two years, he came to be recognized as the leader of all groups that were opposing Batista. Besieged on all sides and abandoned by the United States, Batista fled the country in 1959. Castro took control of the government.

A New Dictatorship Although Castro had promised to restore democracy to Cuba, he established a Communist regime and named himself premier. He executed about 800 former government officials. He seized the property of all foreign corporations. He also established close ties with the Soviet Union. These actions prompted the United States to break off diplomatic relations with Cuba. The United States even banned all trade with Cuba. This trade embargo was still in effect more than 30 years later.

After Castro assumed power, thousands of Cuban refugees migrated to the United States. In April of 1961, a team of U.S.-backed Cuban refugees staged an armed invasion of Cuba in an attempt to overthrow Castro. The invasion, called the Bay of Pigs after the landing site, failed miserably. The force was captured, discrediting the United States.

Cuba in the Cold War The following year, the Soviet Union began to station nuclear missiles on Cuba, only

The U.S. embargo on trade with Cuba and the end of aid from the Soviet Union have drastically reduced Cuba's income. Unable to afford gasoline for cars, many Cubans now use bicycles to travel.

90 miles from the U.S. mainland. For 13 days in October, the world stood on the brink of nuclear war. President John F. Kennedy faced off with Soviet premier Nikita Khrushchev, finally forcing him to remove the missiles. This incident in U.S.-Cuban relations became known as the Cuban Missile Crisis.

Cuba was the first Communist state in the Western Hemisphere, but Castro hoped it would not be the last. He tried to export Communist revolution to other Latin American countries. He aided movements in Haiti, Nicaragua, Colombia, and Panama.

After Castro's Revolution

After more than 30 years, Castro remains the iron-fisted ruler of Cuba. His efforts to export communism to Latin America have largely failed. Cuba is still isolated from the rest of the Western Hemisphere. However, Castro gained recognition on the world stage as a major Third World leader. He has defeated all U.S. efforts to undermine him. And he continues to encourage Communists in other Third World nations to take up arms. He sent Cuban troops to Angola and Ethiopia in the 1970s to support Communist revolutions unfolding there.

At home, Castro made significant strides by expanding health care and education for his people. But the nation's economy remains very poor. The breakup of the Soviet Union and the collapse of communism in Europe were major setbacks for Castro. Concerned with their own economic problems, the former Communist states no longer provide foreign aid to Cuba. Castro has begun to seek new trading partners and to promote tourism to revive the economy.

Low living standards and the repressive government have made many Cubans unhappy. Thousands flee the island each year. It is unclear whether Castro's revolution will survive him.

Mikhail Gorbachev and Castro celebrate the signing of a friendship treaty in 1989. Castro now rules one of the world's few remaining Communist countries.

Martin Luther King, Jr.

He used nonviolence to help win civil rights for black Americans and end racial segregation.

As Gandhi had before him, King (*pointing*) used nonviolent marches to protest unjust treatment. He is shown here leading a civil rights march.

Violence threatened to erupt when black students tried to attend the public schools in Little Rock, Arkansas. King worked hard to end segregation.

Separate but Equal?

After the Civil War, America's former black slaves were given the rights of citizenship enjoyed by whites. However, in the defeated South, where most blacks lived, states passed laws to keep blacks legally segregated. Black children had to attend separate schools. Black people had to use separate hotels, restaurants, parks, movie theaters, drinking fountains, and restrooms.

By the mid-1950s, however, the situation had begun to change. In 1954, the United States Supreme Court issued a historic decision against segregated public schools.

The following year, a black woman in Alabama, Rosa Parks, was arrested for refusing to give up her seat on a bus to a white passenger. These two events marked the beginning of the civil rights movement.

The man who emerged to lead this movement was Martin Luther King, Jr. King was born in Atlanta, Georgia, in 1929, the son and grandson of Baptist ministers. He was a gifted student who entered the all-black Morehouse College at the age of 15. After graduation, he attended a Baptist seminary to study for the ministry, then earned a Ph.D. in theology at Boston University.

King's Career

Montgomery Boycott In 1954, King became the pastor at the Dexter Avenue Baptist Church in Montgomery, Alabama. Following Rosa Parks's arrest, black leaders in the city formed the Montgomery Improvement Association to organize a bus boycott, a refusal to use city buses until they became integrated. They chose King to lead the organization and the protest for several reasons. King was still new in town and had not made enemies among the white establishment. He was well respected, and his family connections would enable him to find another job if the boycott failed. The young minister's eloquence and leadership during the successful, year-long boycott made him a hero in the black community. It also brought him—and the civil rights movement—national attention.

Building on the success of the boycott, King

- Formed the Southern Christian Leadership Conference (SCLC)—a broad-based organization of church groups dedicated to working for civil rights for blacks.

- Lectured throughout the country about civil rights and the second-class citizenship of African Americans.

- Led mass marches against discrimination throughout the South.

**. . . I have a dream
that one day on the red hills of Georgia,
sons of former slaves and sons of former slave owners
will be able to sit down together at the table of brotherhood.
I have a dream
that one day even the state of Mississippi,
a state sweltering with the heat of injustice [and] oppression,
will be transformed into an oasis of freedom and justice.
I have a dream
that my four little children will one day live in a nation
where they will not be judged by the color of their skin
but by the content of their character.**

—excerpt from speech
August 28, 1963

His goals were to integrate public facilities and to win voting rights for African Americans.

In Gandhi's Footsteps In all of his campaigns, King followed Gandhi's example of nonviolent protest. King was arrested 29 times, his house was firebombed, and he received repeated death threats. Dozens of civil rights workers were murdered; others were attacked with fire hoses, police dogs, and clubs. These harsh attacks contrasted dramatically with the nonviolence of King's followers. Many whites, outraged by the violence against King, joined his crusade. King received the Nobel Peace Prize for his use of nonviolent resistance in his campaign for civil rights.

King's career reached a high point in Washington, D.C., on August 28, 1963. On that day, he delivered his famous "I have a dream" speech to more than 250,000 people. Listeners wept when he ended his speech quoting an old spiritual: "Free at last! Free at last! Thank God Almighty, we are free at last!" The following year Congress enacted the Civil Rights Act of 1964, a sweeping federal law that outlawed the racial segregation of public facilities and discrimination in employment.

Full Equality King then led a march from Selma to Montgomery, Alabama, to support a bill for black voting rights. That bill, the Voting Rights Act of 1965, outlawed discriminatory practices that had been widely used to prevent African Americans from registering to vote.

These new laws resulted in full political equality for blacks. For the first time since Reconstruction, the period immediately after the Civil War, blacks and whites were equal before the law.

King began to broaden his following and take on other causes—poverty, housing discrimination, and opposition to the Vietnam War. In 1968, while organizing a sanitation workers' strike in Memphis, Tennessee, he was shot and killed by a racist fanatic. His murderer, James Earl Ray, was sentenced to 99 years in prison.

King's Legacy

The civil rights movement resulted in significant social, economic, and political gains for many blacks. Antipoverty programs in the 1960s and 1970s helped raise the standard of living for many. Affirmative action programs required employers to hire and promote more minorities and provided greater educational opportunities for blacks in colleges and universities. Across the nation African Americans ran successfully for public office, particularly at the state and local levels. However, despite the gains of the civil rights movement, King's dream of total equality and opportunity for black Americans has not yet been fulfilled.

Martin Luther King, Jr., became an important national hero. In 1983, Congress declared his birthday a national holiday. King is the only nonpresident to receive this honor. He is still revered as an advocate of brotherhood.

King's work led to the passage of the Voting Rights Act in 1965, which enabled more blacks to vote. In 1992, Carol Moseley Braun became the first African American woman to win a seat in the U.S. Senate.

31

Anwar Sadat and Menachem Begin

The Egyptian and Israeli leaders sought peace between their countries after decades of hatred and warfare.

The Arab-Israeli Conflict

During the 1800s, small numbers of European Jews migrated to Palestine to escape persecution. The Jews were returning to the land they had been forced to leave almost 2,000 years earlier. However, Arabs, too, called Palestine their home. Arabs and Jews lived together peacefully as long as the number of Jewish immigrants remained small.

A Jewish Homeland When Adolf Hitler came to power in Germany in 1933 and threatened the safety of Jews living there, the number of Jewish people fleeing Europe for Palestine rose significantly. Tension between Arabs and Jews increased, often to the point of violence. After World War II, the growing tide of Jewish immigrants

In winning the 1967 war, Israel seized land from Arab states. Sadat and Begin's peace gave the Sinai Peninsula back to Egypt.

swelled to a flood. The United Nations established the Jewish state of Israel (formerly Palestine) on May 14, 1948. The following day, Israel was attacked by the surrounding Arab countries. Israel found itself fighting for its life against its neighbors. Israel won the 1948 war, increasing its territory by half. The defeated Arab states refused to absorb the half million Palestinian refugees left homeless by the war.

Periodic Wars Tensions remained high between Israel and its neighbors. War erupted again in 1956 and in 1967. During the 1967 war, the Israelis took the West Bank of the Jordan River from Jordan, the Golan Heights from Syria, and the Sinai Peninsula and Gaza Strip from Egypt. Even more Palestinians were now without a country, a sore point for the Arab leaders. The Palestine Liberation Organization (PLO) arose to help regain Palestinian lands. When the PLO attacked Israeli civilians, the Israelis retaliated.

The Careers of Sadat and Begin

Anwar Sadat was an Egyptian Army officer and nationalist who helped make Egypt an independent nation. He joined the Free Officers Committee opposing British control of Egypt. They staged a coup in 1952. They deposed King Farouk, a puppet of the British, and installed an army colonel, Gamal Abdel Nasser, as the head of the government. Sadat served in several posts in Nasser's government, rising to vice-president. When Nasser died suddenly in 1970, Sadat was elected president. He enjoyed great popularity because he promised to wage a new war against Israel.

Menachem Begin was born in Poland in 1913. He studied law at the University of Warsaw in the 1930s. At the same time he became involved in the movement to establish a Jewish homeland in Palestine. During World War II, Begin entered the Free Polish Army exiled in London and was sent

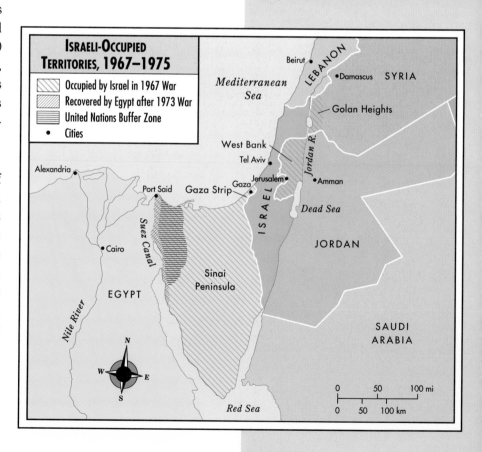

ISRAELI-OCCUPIED TERRITORIES, 1967–1975

- Occupied by Israel in 1967 War
- Recovered by Egypt after 1973 War
- United Nations Buffer Zone
- Cities

to the Middle East. There he joined in the fight for a Jewish state.

When Israel became a nation in 1948, Begin was elected chairman of the Herut Party. For years, he led the conservative opposition to the dominant Labor Party in the Knesset (parliament). In 1973, however, Begin became the leader of a coalition of conservative parties called Likud. In 1977, Likud had enough votes in the Knesset to make Begin prime minister.

The Yom Kippur War In October 1973, Egypt and Syria began a *jihad,* or "holy war," against Israel on the Jewish holy day of Yom Kippur. Israel recovered from early losses to defeat both armies again. But Sadat won a measure of respect by regaining part of the Sinai Peninsula.

An Historic Peace Several years after the war, Sadat surprised the world by offering to travel to Israel to discuss peace. In 1977, Sadat made his historic trip to Israel, the first such visit by any Arab leader. He even spoke to the Knesset to outline his peace proposals.

By 1978, however, the peace talks had reached an impasse. Tensions were again mounting in the Middle East. U.S. President Jimmy Carter invited Anwar Sadat and Menachem Begin to Camp David, the presidential retreat in Maryland, to try to break the deadlock. For nearly two weeks, the two sides argued. Finally they reached an agreement on a peace treaty, now called the Camp David Accords. Israel agreed to give back the Sinai Peninsula except for the Gaza Strip. Egypt agreed to allow Israeli ships to use the Suez Canal.

The peace between a Muslim nation and Israel was historic. The following year Begin and Sadat were jointly awarded the Nobel Peace Prize. But the peace was only partial. Still unmet were Arab demands for Israel to return other Arab territories it occupied and for the creation of a separate homeland for the Palestinians.

Israeli settlements on the West Bank of the Jordan River are a major obstacle to a lasting peace between Israel and its Arab neighbors.

After Camp David

The Arab world reacted with rage to the Camp David treaty. It expelled Egypt from a union called the Arab League and imposed harsh sanctions, or penalties, against it. In 1981, Sadat was assassinated by Muslim fanatics while he was watching a military parade. Menachem Begin resigned as prime minister in 1983 and lived in retirement until his death in 1992.

The peace between Egypt and Israel has continued for more than a decade. But Begin's successors and Arab leaders showed little desire to continue the peace process. Finally, at the urging of the United States and the Soviet Union, the Arab states and Israel agreed to meet in Madrid in October 1991 to begin peace talks. This marked the first time that all major parties, including the Palestinians, were at the negotiating table. The talks continued on and off throughout 1992, largely as a payback for U.S. aid during the Persian Gulf War. The issues of the occupied territories and the fate of the Palestinian refugees remain the major roadblocks to Arab-Israeli peace today.

U.S. President Jimmy Carter looks on as Begin (*left*) and Sadat (*right*) shake hands after agreeing to a peace treaty. Their agreement stunned the world and gave it hope.

Ayatollah Ruhollah Khomeini

As the religious leader of Iran, he overthrew the Shah and led an Islamic revolution that affected politics throughout the Middle East.

Khomeini wielded great power. Millions of Iranians idolized the ayatollah and regarded him as their spiritual leader.

Rule of the Shah

In recent centuries, Iran (formerly Persia) has been dominated by foreign nations. Britain and Russia competed for power in Iran during the 19th and early 20th centuries. In 1925, an Iranian army officer, Reza Khan, seized power and declared himself Shah, or hereditary ruler. The new shah embarked on a program to modernize Iran as a secular, or nonreligious, state. Many of his reforms were aimed at reducing the power of the Muslim clergy, who controlled much of Iranian society. Reza Khan's son, Mohammed Reza Pahlavi, became Shah in 1941. He continued his father's policies. However, he was a harsh ruler, whose

hated secret police routinely tortured and murdered opponents.

Among these opponents was Ruhollah Khomeini. Born in Iran in 1900, Khomeini received a religious education in Muslim schools and became a teacher of religion and philosophy. In the 1950s, he received the religious title of ayatollah. He gained a sizable following by criticizing the shah for abandoning Islam and promoting Western culture in Iran. Khomeini was arrested in 1963 and went into exile, first in Iraq, then in France. During his exile, he continued to direct the movement to overthrow the shah by smuggling inspirational tapes to his followers.

The Islamic Revolution

Nationwide strikes, demonstrations, and riots forced Shah Pahlavi to flee the country in January 1979. Khomeini triumphantly returned from exile two weeks later. He organized a new Islamic republic with himself as its religious and political leader. He then "retired" to the city of Qum. There he directed the new revolutionary government's efforts to remove influences of Western culture and revive Islamic traditions. Western music and alcohol were banned. Women were forced to wear the *chador,* the traditional long black dress of Islamic women.

34

A year after Khomeini's death, women still mourn. The sign reads, "The brokenhearted have endured one year of loss, but how can they endure a whole lifetime of loss?"

► Angered by U.S. actions, Iranian militants stormed the U.S. embassy in Tehran and took 52 Americans as hostages. The plight of the hostages ultimately affected the 1980 presidential elections.

Rule of the Clergy Khomeini and his followers established a new government based on Islamic law. Religious courts sentenced offenders to harsh punishments in accordance with ancient Islamic law. Revolutionary courts executed or imprisoned thousands of the shah's government officials. They were accused of corruption, serving in the shah's secret police, or promoting pro-Western policies. The courts also persecuted members of minority religions including Christians, Baha'is, and Jews. Ultimately, Khomeini's goal was not just to create a fundamentalist Islamic state in Iran. He wanted to spread his revolution throughout the Muslim world.

In his relations with the non-Muslim world, Khomeini took a neutral stand. He turned his back on both the democracies of Western Europe and the Communist bloc. However, he harbored a special hatred for the United States, which he called "the Great Satan," because it had supported the shah for many years. When the exiled shah entered the United States for medical treatment in 1979, angry student militants took over the U.S. embassy in Tehran. With Khomeini's approval, they held 50 American embassy employees hostage for more than 14 months. President Carter's inability to rescue the hostages or to secure their release through diplomatic means embarrassed the United States. It also contributed to Carter's failure to win reelection. After revealing America's powerlessness to the world, the student militants finally released the hostages.

War with Iraq In 1980, Iraq invaded Iran in a dispute over territory. The war lasted eight years and took more than a million lives. By the mid-1980s, the conflict had expanded to involve Saudi Arabia, Kuwait, and other Persian Gulf states. These countries, dependent on oil trade with the West, disliked Khomeini's revolution. When both Iran and Iraq attacked oil tankers in the Persian Gulf, the United States, Britain, and France sent warships to protect oil shipments. The Iran-Iraq War ended in a stalemate in 1988. Khomeini died a year later.

After Khomeini

The war left Iran in economic ruin from which it is only beginning to recover. After Khomeini's death, Iran's political leadership was divided between his followers and more moderate leaders. The moderates wanted to reestablish ties with the Western industrial nations. The new leadership has turned away slightly from Khomeini's rigid policies. It has relaxed some of the strict rules regarding behavior and dress. It has also begun to make contact with other nations, including the United States. In 1990, a major earthquake killed 35,000 Iranians and left nearly half a million homeless. Iran accepted aid from the United States.

Khomeini was widely admired and deeply mourned by millions of Muslims. He inspired fundamentalist movements in many Arab states. In some of these states, Muslims are seriously challenging the pro-Western policies of their national leaders. The force of this religious revival will affect Middle East politics for many years to come.

Margaret Thatcher

Nicknamed "the Iron Lady," she led Great Britain away from the socialist policies of the welfare state.

Thatcher served longer than any other British prime minister in the 20th century. She is shown here with the leaders of the major Western economic powers.

Britain's Ailing Economy

In the 1970s, Great Britain was hard hit by a global and national recession. It suffered from high unemployment and the highest rate of inflation of all the Western industrial nations. In addition, Britain's powerful trade unions staged a series of strikes and walkouts that further weakened the nation's economy. At the same time, Britain was developing closer economic and political ties with the European Economic Community (EEC), a move that many British Conservatives opposed.

The daughter of a prosperous grocer, Margaret Thatcher was fiercely proud of her English heritage, especially its traditions of independence and self-reliance. She attended Oxford University, where she earned degrees in chemistry and law. While at Oxford, she served as the first woman president of the university's Conservative Club. Thatcher won election to Parliament as a Conservative Party candidate in 1959. She dedicated herself to changing the policies of Britain's postwar socialist governments. She believed those policies had created a welfare state and caused the country's economic problems.

A Woman Prime Minister

Taking advantage of disunity in the Conservative Party, Margaret Thatcher took over its leadership in the mid-1970s. In 1979, the Conservatives handily defeated the foundering Labour Party in national elections. Thatcher, as head of the party, became the first woman prime minister in Europe. Known for her toughness and her unwillingness to compromise, Thatcher soon earned the nickname "the Iron Lady." Early in her first term, she declared, "I am not a consensus politician, I'm a conviction politician," meaning that she did what she believed was right whether or not her actions pleased others.

A New Conservatism Thatcher embarked on a program of economic recovery that included:

- cutting government spending,
- reducing taxation,
- curbing imports,
- curtailing the power of the labor unions,
- encouraging private enterprise and investments, and
- holding down wages.

Thatcher sold to private owners nearly one-third of Britain's state-owned businesses, such as electric, gas, and water companies. The reductions in government spending hurt public education and national health care. Nevertheless, Thatcher became popular with many working-class Britons because she enabled more than one million people to purchase their formerly government-owned homes. Under her leadership, the very nature of British conservatism changed. In the past, Britain's wealthy, aristocratic Conservatives had taken a paternalistic, or protective, attitude toward the lower classes. Thatcher's new conservatism now stood for capitalism and a free market economy. She saw private-sector jobs, not government handouts, as the way to help the poor.

Thatcher's policies reduced inflation and made Britain's industries more profitable. But they also produced high levels of unemployment. In addition, tax policies that favored wealthy investors and business owners widened the gap between the rich

◀ Thatcher's economic policies brought her into conflict with striking miners and other trade union members. As this political cartoon shows, "the Iron Lady" often won.

▼ In addition to high unemployment in the mid-1980s, Thatcher's economic policies resulted in increased interest rates, a trade deficit, and high levels of homelessness.

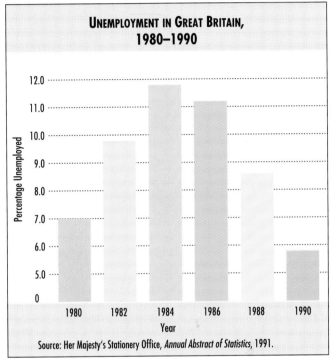

UNEMPLOYMENT IN GREAT BRITAIN, 1980–1990

Source: Her Majesty's Stationery Office, *Annual Abstract of Statistics*, 1991.

and poor. Meanwhile, nonwhite immigrants from Britain's former colonies poured into Great Britain to compete with native-born whites for scarce jobs. These factors increased racial and ethnic tensions, resulting in riots in several major cities in the spring and summer of 1981.

The Falklands War Thatcher's popularity had plummeted to an all-time low by the end of 1981. Even Conservatives began to turn against her economic policies. Four months later, Argentina claimed the Falkland Islands, British possessions that lay a few hundred miles off Argentina's coast. When Argentina invaded the islands, Thatcher sent an enormous British force. The Falklands were back in British hands within two months, and Thatcher rode a wave of patriotism and popularity back into office in 1983.

Thatcher cultivated a close friendship with the United States and remained a firm supporter of NATO, the U.S.-European mutual defense organization. However, she strongly opposed the European Economic Community's movement toward becoming one supernation with its own government, money, and economy.

Popularity Plummets

In 1985 Thatcher replaced property taxes with a very unpopular "poll tax," to fund local government. The poll tax, Thatcher's continuing opposition to European unity, and a new economic downturn caused her popularity to plummet once again in the late 1980s. She was forced to resign as head of the party and prime minister in 1990.

Thatcher served as prime minister for 11 years, longer than any other British leader in the 20th century. During her term in office, she changed the face of British politics. She managed to curb the welfare state that had grown for decades and to promote individual initiative. The Labour Party was so badly damaged during her administration that many moderate Labourites left their party to form a new party, the Social Democrats.

Her critics say that "Thatcherism" gutted the nation's social services system, especially damaging education and national health programs. However, Thatcher's unpopular policies did not prevent another Conservative, John Major, from succeeding her. In departing from her policies, Major sought additional funding for health and education. He also moved to strengthen ties with the European Economic Community. But the Thatcher policy of promoting capitalism and downplaying the welfare state seemed firmly rooted.

Lech Walesa

◆

By challenging Poland's Communist government, he contributed to the fall of communism throughout Eastern Europe.

▲ In the 1980s, Solidarity's banner became a symbol of hope for freedom in Communist Eastern Europe.

◀ Workers at the Gdansk shipyard carried strike leader Walesa on their shoulders as they celebrated the signing of an agreement between the union and the Polish government in 1980.

State-Controlled Poland

Nazi Germany had occupied Poland throughout World War II, until the Germans were driven out by advancing troops from the Soviet Union. After Germany's defeat, Poland became a Soviet satellite nation along with the other nations of Eastern Europe. The Soviets replaced Poland's prewar political leaders with a Soviet-trained Communist government loyal to Moscow. Under the new regime, businesses and industries were taken over by the state. Political freedom was suspended as the Communist Party took control of all governmental institutions. The Communists also curtailed religious freedom in Poland, an overwhelmingly Roman Catholic country.

Lech Walesa was born in Nazi-occupied Poland in 1943. He attended a state vocational school and then found work as an electrician at the huge Lenin Shipyard in Gdansk. Walesa first became a political activist in 1970 when he took part in the "bread riots." That protest against rising food prices was brutally suppressed by the government.

The Rise of Solidarity

Lech Walesa represented the workers at the Lenin Shipyard in a state-sponsored trade union. In 1976, when he drew up a list of workers' grievances, he was fired from his job. He went to work for a machine shop and continued fighting for workers' rights. Two years later, he founded the Baltic Free Trades Union Movement, which sought the right to establish unions that were free from state control.

In 1980, another increase in food prices set off a series of strikes throughout the country. Workers at the Lenin Shipyard demanded the reinstatement of Walesa and other union leaders. Walesa boldly scaled the fence enclosing the shipyard to rejoin his former coworkers and become the strike leader. Within a few weeks the Polish government, threatened with nationwide rebellion, negotiated an agreement with Walesa that gave workers the right to form an independent union and to strike over economic issues. The agreement

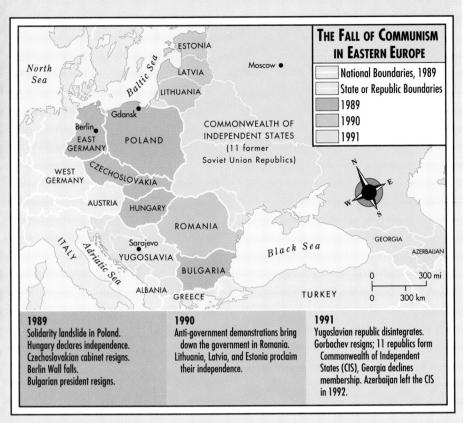

THE FALL OF COMMUNISM IN EASTERN EUROPE

	National Boundaries, 1989
	State or Republic Boundaries
	1989
	1990
	1991

1989
Solidarity landslide in Poland.
Hungary declares independence.
Czechoslovakian cabinet resigns.
Berlin Wall falls.
Bulgarian president resigns.

1990
Anti-government demonstrations bring
down the government in Romania.
Lithuania, Latvia, and Estonia proclaim
their independence.

1991
Yugoslavian republic disintegrates.
Gorbachev resigns; 11 republics form
Commonwealth of Independent
States (CIS), Georgia declines
membership. Azerbaijan left the CIS
in 1992.

After more than four decades of Communist rule in Eastern Europe, 1989 began years of upheaval. By 1991, even the Soviet Union had rejected communism.

also promised higher wages and better benefits to the workers. Walesa and his followers formed a coalition of independent unions that they called "Solidarity." Within a few years, Solidarity's membership grew to more than 10 million industrial and agricultural workers.

Walesa Imprisoned Encouraged by Solidarity's victory, the workers continued to strike. They now demanded free elections and greater participation in government. The Soviet Union, in an effort to support Poland's Communist government, threatened to send troops and tanks to Poland. In 1981, Poland's premier, General Wojciech Jaruzelski, declared martial law, suspended all civil rights, and sent troops to end the strikes. The following year, Jaruzelski's police arrested Walesa and other Solidarity leaders. The government outlawed Solidarity.

Lech Walesa was released from prison in less than two months, but the government continued to harass him. Solidarity leaders secretly continued their campaign for economic and political reforms. The economy remained stagnant for the next eight years while Poland's work force remained resentful and rebellious.

Nobel Peace Prize In the meantime, people all over the world came to admire and support Lech Walesa and the Solidarity movement. In 1983, Walesa was awarded the Nobel Peace Prize for his work with Solidarity. The prize committee said of him, "he stands as an inspiration and a shining example to all those . . . who fight for freedom and humanity." Finally, the country's deepening economic crisis forced Jaruzelski to invite Walesa to Warsaw for a series of peace talks. The negotiations resulted in an agreement to legalize Solidarity and allow it to participate in partially free elections. Those talks marked the beginning of the end of Communist government in Poland.

The Triumph of Solidarity

Although Solidarity was created to improve the economic condition of Poland's workers, it soon included demands for participation in government as well. In 1989, Solidarity candidates were allowed to stand for election to a limited number of seats in the new parliament. Solidarity won in nearly all of the contested races—those in which Solidarity candidates ran against Communist candidates. The Communists even lost many of the races in which they ran unopposed. This was because voters simply crossed their names off the ballot. The result of Solidarity's landslide victory was that the Communist Party became a minority party and was forced to form a coalition cabinet with Solidarity. Communism came to a peaceful end in Poland after more than 40 years of totalitarian rule. Solidarity played a crucial role in toppling communism not only in Poland but also throughout Eastern Europe.

In 1990, Walesa was elected president of Poland. The newly free nation faces many problems including low productivity, high prices, rundown factories, and massive emigration of Poles to the West. Poland is trying to get Western investment to help rebuild the economy.

Mikhail Gorbachev

As leader of the Soviet Union, he tried to reform the Communist system but witnessed, instead, the collapse of the USSR.

The Need for Reform

The Soviet Union was established soon after Bolshevik revolutionaries overthrew the Russian czar, Nicholas II. The Communist dictatorship they set up ruled Russia and more than a dozen adjoining lands in central Asia and Eastern Europe for 70 years. In the late 1940s, the Soviet Union extended its grip to control additional Eastern European countries as well.

By the 1980s, however, the Soviet Union's state-run economy had fallen into a steady decline:

- Industrial output was lagging.
- Consumer goods were shoddy, expensive, and scarce.
- People were angered by the lack of consumer goods.
- People resented the corruption within the Communist Party.

In the early 1980s, the Soviet Union had three national leaders in rapid succession. Each was old, and each died shortly after assuming power. The Politburo, or executive branch, then chose its youngest member, Mikhail Gorbachev, to take over as the party's general secretary.

A New Party Leader The son of peasants, Gorbachev earned a law degree in 1955 and began a career in politics as an expert on agriculture. He rapidly worked his way up through Communist Party ranks, becoming a voting member of the Politburo in 1980. As the minister for agriculture, Gorbachev enjoyed considerable power and responsibility. He quickly gained a reputation as a persuasive speaker, leader, and statesman.

Although firmly committed to communism, Gorbachev saw the need to reform the system. His appointment as head of the party also made him the leader of the country.

Unlike previous Soviet leaders, Gorbachev understood the interdependence of the nations of the world. He was eager to work with other leaders to achieve peace and security for all.

An Era of Reform

Gorbachev knew that his most urgent task was to restructure the Soviet Union's faltering economy. To gain public support for economic changes, he realized, he also had to permit political reforms. He soon introduced a policy of *glasnost,* or "openness," to encourage new ideas and debate. The following changes occurred:

- Government censorship ended.
- Political dissidents were released from prison.
- Freedom of speech and press were allowed.
- Freedom of religion was restored.

After decades of repression, the Soviet people were finally able to speak their minds.

Gorbachev then announced his economic plan, which he called *perestroika,* or "restructuring." He

◀ Gorbachev's skillful diplomacy helped to reduce nuclear arms in the world. He is shown here with U.S. President Ronald Reagan exchanging treaty documents in 1987.

With the fall of communism came the toppling of its symbols. Thousands cheered as the statue of the founder of the Soviet secret police was brought down.

Changes After Gorbachev

In 1991, one Soviet republic after another declared its independence from the Soviet Union. As the USSR stood on the brink of collapse, a group of faithful Communists seized Gorbachev in a desperate attempt to restore Communist rule. Boris Yeltsin, the head of the Russian Republic, bravely stood up to the tanks that were sent to take over the Russian legislature. By rallying the people and helping to defeat the coup, Yeltsin became a popular hero and the most powerful leader in all of the newly independent republics.

Gorbachev's career was finished. Remaining loyal to the Communist Party, he was left with no role to play in the new order. He resigned, and the Soviet Union ceased to exist.

Boris Yeltsin continued as the head of the Russian Republic. But economic disorder and ethnic violence in several of the new nations leave his future and the future of the democratic reforms in doubt.

proposed removing the economy from state control and allowing farm and factory workers to manage themselves. He hoped to eliminate the many rules that bureaucrats wrote to control the economy. The economy was made more open:

- Factories were to show a profit.
- Individuals would be able to start their own businesses.
- Foreign investment was encouraged.

But state bureaucrats opposed perestroika, and Gorbachev was reluctant to move ahead without their support.

Gorbachev also introduced democracy to the Soviet Union. He allowed regional and local soviets, or governing committees, more authority to make their own decisions. The Supreme Soviet, the national legislature, which formerly had existed only to rubber-stamp Politburo decisions, became a real legislature. Members of the Soviet were now able to propose, debate, and enact laws.

In 1989, the Soviet Union held partially free elections. Non-Communists and dissidents were elected to a new body, the Congress of People's Deputies. They, in turn, chose the members of the Supreme Soviet. Their selections included a sizable number of non-Communists, reflecting people's desire to break the Communist stranglehold on power. The following year, the Congress voted to end the one-party system. Boris Yeltsin, a popular and outspoken Russian, was one of the new leaders elected by the people.

Communism Collapses While perestroika was blocked and the economy continued its slump, the political reforms worked all too well. Three Baltic nations that the Soviet Union had seized in 1940 began to demand their freedom from Soviet control. Lithuania declared its independence in 1990, followed by Estonia and Latvia.

People in the Communist nations of Eastern Europe were demanding government changes as well. Gorbachev, to the world's surprise, did not stop them. As a result, the people of Poland, East Germany, Czechoslovakia, Yugoslavia, and Romania were able to overthrow their Communist dictators. Gorbachev also ended the arms race between the United States and the Soviet Union. His reforms at home and diplomacy abroad helped to end the Cold War and to free the world from the threat of nuclear war.

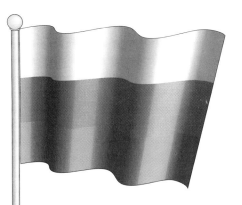

The new flag of Russia flew over the largest of the 15 nations that rose from the collapsed USSR.

Nelson Mandela

The imprisoned black leader led the civil rights struggle for all people in racially divided South Africa.

A South African mother and her son sit among their belongings after a mining company has bulldozed the shacks of three hundred blacks living in the area.

Rule of the Minority

South Africa is a nation consisting of 16 million blacks and 5 million whites. Another 3 million South Africans are of mixed race (called coloreds) or Asians. South Africa was settled first by the Dutch (Boers) in the 18th century and then conquered by the English in the 19th century. The Boers resisted British rule and almost defeated a powerful British army in the Boer War (1899–1902). But the British rebounded and created the Union of South Africa in 1910.

South Africa's ruling white minority, especially the Boers (increasingly called Afrikaners), had insisted on racial separation. But the nation did not adopt a formal policy of segregation until 1948, when the Afrikaners came to power. The policy is called *apartheid*. It included laws that specified where nonwhites could live, classified South Africans by race at birth, and prohibited nonwhites from voting. The law also allowed the government to arrest and detain nonwhites without trial or access to a lawyer.

Nelson Mandela was born into this racially divided society in 1918. He was the son of the chief of the Tembu tribe, an important South African ethnic group. He gave up his hereditary right to Tembu leadership and left home to avoid an arranged marriage. Mandela attended the University of South Africa and became a lawyer. With colleagues Walter Sisulu and Oliver Tambo, he formed the first black law firm in South Africa. Mandela joined the African National Congress (ANC) in 1944. The ANC is a black nationalist party that was established in 1912 to oppose apartheid.

Prison and Triumph

In 1960, police opened fire on unarmed, antiapartheid demonstrators, killing hundreds of people. The ANC was outlawed and Mandela went underground to continue the fight for political change. Denied the legal means to affect change in the apartheid laws, Mandela established the *Umkhonto we Sizwe,* meaning "spear of the nation." This military wing of the ANC intended to use sabotage and violence to end apartheid.

Mandela was arrested in 1962 and sentenced to five years in prison. The following year, police raided a house in Johannesburg, where they found arms and equipment belonging to Umkhonto. Mandela, with close ties to the organization, was charged with conspiracy to overthrow the government and sentenced to life imprisonment.

Thousands heard Nelson Mandela speak of South Africa's new future at this rally held shortly after his release from prison.

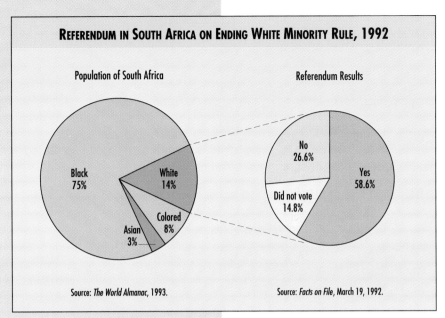

REFERENDUM IN SOUTH AFRICA ON ENDING WHITE MINORITY RULE, 1992

Population of South Africa

Black 75%
White 14%
Colored 8%
Asian 3%

Source: *The World Almanac*, 1993.

Referendum Results

No 26.6%
Yes 58.6%
Did not vote 14.8%

Source: *Facts on File*, March 19, 1992.

Although only 14 percent of the population—the white minority—could vote, they abolished white minority rule in South Africa by a margin of more than two to one.

Symbol of Freedom Mandela spent the next 27 years in prison, most of them under harsh conditions in a maximum-security facility. From prison, Mandela continued to speak out against apartheid and injustice. South Africa's blacks looked to him for inspiration. Individuals, organizations, and governments around the world rallied to his cause and demanded an end to apartheid. In the 1980s, the governments of many nations imposed economic sanctions on South Africa, refusing to trade with or invest in the country. Recognizing the strength of Mandela's leadership, the government twice offered him his freedom on condition that he publicly renounce the use of violence in his struggle against apartheid. But Mandela refused both times because no changes to apartheid were offered.

A New Beginning The economic sanctions had resulted in a stagnant economy and high unemployment in South Africa. By the late 1980s, the government realized that drastic action was needed to end racial conflict and get the economy going again. It entered into three years of secret talks with Mandela, the imprisoned ANC leader.

Finally in 1990, the government lifted its ban on the ANC and recognized it as a legitimate political party once again. Three days later, Nelson Mandela was released from prison. The 71-year-old Mandela, with white hair, walked through the gates, his clenched fists held high in the air. Tens of thousands of people gathered to hear him speak that night in Cape Town and two days later in the black township of Soweto.

After Mandela's Release

In a national referendum in 1992, South Africa's white electorate voted to end white minority rule by a margin of more than two to one. Since his release, Mandela and representatives of the ANC and other black groups have worked with President F. W. de Klerk's government to abolish major apartheid laws and to create a new constitution that will include equal rights for all. The world community, meanwhile, has lifted many of its economic sanctions. Foreign investors are eager to invest in South Africa.

Many obstacles still remain, however. Between 1989 and 1992, more than 8,000 blacks were killed in a power struggle between the ANC and its main rival for black support, the Inkatha (Freedom) Party. In addition, South Africa's white minority is demanding protection for itself in any new constitution.

Even though apartheid has been abolished, it will take years for the country's black citizens to catch up economically. South Africa still has a long way to go, says Mandela: "I still cannot vote in my own country."

Glossary

apartheid: The policy of racial segregation, or separation, practiced in South Africa.

Bolsheviks: The group that overthrew the Russian government in November 1917 and became the Communist Party.

boycott: The refusal to use a service or product in order to achieve a desired political goal.

bureaucracy: An elaborate system of government employing many officials.

capitalism: An economic system in which businesses are privately owned and prices are established by competition in a free market.

civil disobedience: The refusal to obey a law one considers unjust.

civil war: A war between two opposing groups within a country.

Cold War: The hostility that existed, without actual fighting, between the United States and the Soviet Union from the end of World War II until the fall of communism in 1990.

colonialism: Control by one nation over people in another land.

communism: The socialist system set up in the Soviet Union according to Marxist principles, in which factories, businesses, and farms were owned and controlled by the state.

concentration camp: A camp where members of a group are confined, such as the camps in which millions of Jews and other persons were murdered in Nazi Germany.

five-year plan: One of a set of goals for increasing industrial production, first used in the Soviet Union.

Great Depression: The period of massive unemployment and business failures that lasted from 1929 until the beginning of World War II.

guerrilla warfare: Attacks by small groups of fighters who are not members of a regular army.

Holocaust: The mass murder of six million Jews, as well as an estimated five million others, that took place in the concentration camps of Nazi Germany.

inflation: The economic condition of rising prices.

iron curtain: The symbolic boundary between communist Eastern Europe and democratic Western Europe that existed from the end of World War II until the fall of communism.

isolationism: The belief that a country should not become involved in the affairs of other nations.

Marxism: The economic theory of Karl Marx predicting that the workers of the world would overthrow the factory owners and establish a socialist society.

nationalist: Working for the independence of a particular nation or cultural group.

neutrality: The avoidance of taking sides in a war.

nonviolent protest: The use of peaceful methods such as strikes, marches, fasts, and boycotts to achieve a political goal.

Progressive movement: The effort by various groups in the early 1900s to fight corruption in government, to end the abuses of big business, and to protect workers and consumers.

proletariat: The urban working class, which according to Marxist theory would establish a worldwide dictatorship.

purge: Removal of one's political enemies by execution or exile.

segregation: Separation of races, either by law or by custom.

settlement house: A neighborhood center, usually in a city, that offers various social services such as child care, health clinics, adult education, and cultural activities.

socialism: Economic system in which the means of production are owned and controlled by the state.

Social Security: The provision of pensions to the elderly or disabled.

soviet: A regional or local governing committee in the Soviet Union.

sweatshop: A factory in which workers are paid low wages to work long hours under unhealthy conditions.

suffrage: The right to vote.

tenement: A city apartment house that barely meets minimum standards of safety and sanitation.

Third World: The poor and underdeveloped countries of the world; originally so called because they did not belong to either the Western nations or the Communist bloc.

totalitarian: Holding complete control over the people of a nation.

welfare state: A country in which the government is responsible for social services such as health care and education.

Suggested Readings

Note: An asterisk (*) denotes a Young Adult title.

Bush, Catherine. *Mohandas K. Gandhi.* Chelsea House, 1985.

Clark, Ronald William. *Lenin.* Harper and Row, 1988.

Clements, Kendrick A. *Woodrow Wilson: World Statesman.* Twayne Publishers, 1987.

Conquest, Robert. *Stalin: Breaker of Nations.* Penguin, 1991.

*Craig, Mary. *Lech Walesa: The Leader of Solidarity and Campaigner for Freedom and Human Rights in Poland.* Gareth Stevens Inc., 1990.

*DeChancie, John. *Gamal Abdel Nasser.* Chelsea House, 1987.

*Dolan, Edward D., and Scarino, Margaret M. *Cuba and the United States.* Franklin Watts, 1987.

*Drieman, J. E. *Winston Churchill: An Unbreakable Spirit.* Dillon, 1990.

*Freedman, Russell. *Franklin Delano Roosevelt.* Clarion Books, 1990.

*Fuchs, Thomas. *The Hitler Fact Book.* Fountain Books, 1990.

*Gernand, Renee. *The Cuban Americans.* Chelsea House, 1989.

*Gordon, Matthew S. *Ayatollah Khomeini.* Chelsea House, 1987.

Harris, Kenneth. *Thatcher.* Little, Brown and Company, 1988.

*Hole, Dorothy. *Margaret Thatcher: Britain's Prime Minister.* Enslow Publishers, Inc., 1990.

*Hughes, Libby. *Madam Prime Minister: A Biography of Margaret Thatcher.* Macmillan, 1989.

*Kittredge, Mary. *Jane Addams.* Chelsea House, 1988.

*Kort, Michael. *Mikhail Gorbachev.* Franklin Watts, 1990.

*Lloyd, Dana Ohlmeyer. *Ho Chi Minh.* Chelsea House, 1986.

Patterson, Lillie, *Martin Luther King, Jr. and the Freedom Movement.* Facts on File, 1988.

Perlmutter, Amos. *The Life and Time of Menachem Begin.* Doubleday and Company, 1987.

*Poole, Frederick King. *Mao Zedong.* Franklin Watts, 1982.

Shivanandan, Mary. *Nasser: Modern Leader of Egypt.* SamHar Press, 1973.

*Stefoff, Rebecca. *Nelson Mandela: A Voice Set Free.* Fawcett Book Group, 1990.

*Sullivan, George. *Mikhail Gorbachev.* Julian Messner, 1988.

*———. *Sadat: The Man Who Changed Mid-East History.* Walker and Company, 1981.

*Wepman, Dennis. *Jomo Kenyatta.* Chelsea House, 1985.

Index

◆